GALATIANS

The Wondrous Grace of God

JOHN MACARTHUR

Galatians

Table of Contents

THE EPISTLE OF PAUL TO THE GALATIANS

Introduction

Galatians derives its title *(pros Galatas)* from the region in Asia Minor (modern Turkey) where the churches addressed were located. This is Paul's only epistle specifically addressed to churches in more than one city (1:2; see 3:1; 1 Corinthians 16:1).

Author and Date

There is no reason to question the internal claims that the apostle Paul wrote Galatians (1:1; 5:2). Paul was born in Tarsus, a city in the province of Cilicia, not far from Galatia. Under the famous rabbi Gamaliel, Paul received a thorough training in the Old Testament Scriptures and in the rabbinic traditions at Jerusalem (Acts 22:3). A member of the ultra-orthodox sect of the Pharisees (Acts 23:6), he was one of first-century Judaism's rising stars (1:14; see Philippians 3:5–6).

The course of Paul's life took a sudden and startling turn when, on his way to Damascus from Jerusalem to persecute Christians, he was confronted by the risen, glorified Christ (see Acts 9). That dramatic encounter turned Paul from Christianity's chief persecutor to its greatest missionary. His three missionary journeys and his trip to Rome turned Christianity from a faith that included only a small group of Palestinian Jewish believers into an empire-wide phenomenon. Galatians is one of thirteen inspired letters that Paul addressed to Gentile congregations or his fellow workers.

Chapter 2 describes Paul's visit to the Jerusalem Council of Acts 15 (see 2:1), so he must have written Galatians after that event. Since most scholars date the Jerusalem Council at about A.D. 49, the most likely date for Galatians is shortly thereafter.

Background and Setting

In Paul's day, the word *Galatia* had two distinct meanings. In a strict ethnic sense, Galatia was the region of central Asia Minor inhabited by the Galatians. They were a Celtic people who had migrated to that region from Gaul (modern France) in the third century B.C. The Romans conquered the Galatians in 189 B.C. but allowed them to have some measure of independence until 25 B.C., when Galatia became a Roman province, incorporating some regions not inhabited by ethnic Galatians (for example, parts of Lycaonia, Phrygia, and Pisidia). In a political sense, Galatia came to describe the entire Roman province, not merely the region inhabited by the ethnic Galatians.

Paul founded churches in the southern Galatian cities of Antioch, Iconium, Lystra, and Derbe (Acts 13:14—14:23). These cities, although within the Roman province of Galatia, were not in the ethnic Galatian region. There is no record of Paul's founding churches in that northern, less populated region.

Those two uses of the word Galatia make it more difficult to determine who the original recipients of the epistle were. Some interpret Galatia in its strict racial sense and argue that Paul addressed this epistle to churches in the northern Galatian region, inhabited by the ethnic descendants of the Gauls. Although the apostle apparently crossed the border into the fringes of ethnic Galatia on at least two occasions (Acts 16:6; 18:23), Acts does not record that he founded any churches or engaged in any evangelistic ministry there.

Because neither Acts nor Galatians mentions any cities or people from northern (ethnic) Galatia, it is reasonable to believe that Paul addressed this epistle to churches located in the southern part of the Roman province, but outside of the ethnic Galatian region. Acts records the apostle's founding of such churches at Pisidian Antioch (Acts 13:14–50), Iconium (Acts 13:51—14:7; see 16:2), Lystra (Acts 14:8–19; see 16:2), and Derbe (Acts 14:20–21; see 16:1). In addition, the churches Paul addressed had apparently been established before the Jerusalem Council (Galatians 2:5), and the churches of southern Galatia fit that criterion, having been founded during Paul's first missionary journey before the Council met. Paul did not visit northern (ethnic) Galatia until after the Jerusalem Council (Acts 16:6).

Paul wrote Galatians to counter Judaizing false teachers who were undermining the central New Testament doctrine of justification by faith (see Romans 3:24). Ignoring the express decree of the Jerusalem Council (Acts 15:23–29), they were spreading a dangerous teaching that Gentiles must first become Jewish proselytes and submit to all the Mosaic law before they could become Christians (Gal. 1:7; 4:17, 21; 5:2–12; 6:12–13). Shocked by the Galatians' openness to that damning heresy (1:6), Paul wrote this letter to defend justification by faith and warn these churches of the dire consequences of abandoning that essential doctrine. Galatians is Paul's only epistle that does not contain a commendation of its readers—this obvious omission reflects how urgently he felt about confronting the defection and defending the essential doctrine of justification.

Historical and Theological Themes

Galatians provides valuable historical information about Paul's background (chapters 1 and 2), that Acts does not mention; including his three-year stay in Nabatean Arabia (1:17–18), his fifteen-day visit with Peter after his stay in Arabia (1:18–19); his trip to the Jerusalem Council (2:1–10); his confrontation of Peter (2:11–21).

As already noted, the central theme of Galatians (like that of Romans) is justification by faith. Paul defends that doctrine (the heart of the gospel) both in its theological (chapters 3 and 4) and practical (chapters 5 and 6) ramifications. Paul also defends his position as an apostle (chapters 1 and 2) since, as in Corinth, false teachers had attempted to gain a hearing for their heretical teaching by undermining his credibility. The main theological themes of Galatians are strikingly similar to those of Romans; for example, the inability of the law to justify (2:16; see Romans 3:20); the believer's deadness to the law (Galatians 2:19; see Romans 7:4); the believer's crucifixion with Christ (2:20; see Romans 6:6); Abraham's justification by faith (3:6; see Romans 4:3); believers as Abraham's spiritual children (3:7; see Romans 4:10–11) and therefore blessed (3:9; see Romans 4:23–24); the law bringing not salvation but God's wrath (3:10; see Romans 4:15); the just living by faith (3:11; see Romans 1:17); the universality of sin (3:22; see Romans 11:32); believers as spiritually baptized into Christ (3:27; see Romans 6:3); believers adopted as God's spiritual children (4:5–7; see Romans 8:14–17); love fulfilling the law (5:14; see Romans 13:8–10); the importance of walking in the Spirit (5:16; see Romans 8:4); the warfare of the flesh against the Spirit (5:17; see Romans

7:23, 25); the importance of believers bearing one another's burdens (6:2; see Romans 15:1).

Interpretive Challenges

First, Paul described a visit to Jerusalem and a subsequent meeting with Peter, James, and John (2:1–10). The text contains a question to be resolved, as to whether that was Paul's visit to the Jerusalem Council (Acts 15), or his earlier visit bringing famine relief to the Jerusalem church (Acts 11:27–30).

Second, those who teach baptismal regeneration (the false doctrine that baptism is necessary for salvation) support their view from Gal. 3:27.

Third, some have used this epistle to support their attacks on the biblical roles of men and women, claiming that the spiritual equality taught in 3:28 is incompatible with the traditional concept of authority and submission.

Fourth, those who reject the doctrine of eternal security argue that the phrase "you have fallen from grace" (5:4) describes believers who lost their salvation.

Fifth, there is disagreement whether Paul's statement "See with what large letters I have written to you with my own hand!" refers to the entire letter or merely the concluding verses.

Finally, many claim that Paul erased the line between Israel and the church when he identified the church as the "Israel of God" (6:16).

These challenges will be addressed in the notes to the appropriate passages.

Departing from the Gospel

Opening Thought

1) A common question asked by many evangelists when speaking to people about their spiritual condition is this: "Suppose you were to die today and you suddenly found yourself standing before the heavenly gates. God Himself met you there and asked, 'Why should I let you into heaven?' What response would you give?"

_____

_____

_____

_____

What are some of the most common replies people give to this question?

_____

_____

_____

_____

2) What would *you* say?

_____

_____

_____

_____

_____

Background of the Passage

The gospel of Jesus Christ is good news to rebellious creatures facing the righteous judgment of a holy God. It is, in fact, the best news ever announced. The gospel liberates. It transforms. It saves.

This unearthly message of deliverance and hope changed the apostle Paul's life and radically redirected him. The transformation in Paul was so thorough that this former enemy of the gospel committed his life to traveling the known world to tell his marvelous story to anyone and everyone who would listen.

On his first missionary journey, Paul journeyed through Galatia (modern-day Turkey) preaching and establishing churches. Within a very short time, however, a number of prominent Jewish legalists infiltrated these grace communities and began teaching that faith in Christ alone was not enough to make a person right with God. Salvation, according to their convincing arguments, also required strict adherence to the Mosaic law.

The result was confused congregations and, ultimately, an angry apostle. Paul's deep concern over the churches' defection from the gospel is evident from the opening paragraphs of this letter, which lacks his customary commendations and courtesies and is, instead, brief and impersonal, with a sharp tone.

Is the purity of the gospel important? Is it all right to take an eclectic approach to spirituality—to mix elements of radically different faith traditions with the message of grace in Christ? Paul answers with a resounding "No!"

Bible Passage

Read 1:1–9, noting the key words and definitions to the right of the passage.

Galatians 1:1–9

¹ *Paul, an apostle (not from men nor through man, but through Jesus Christ and God the Father who raised Him from the dead),*

² *and all the brethren who are with me, to the churches of Galatia:*

apostle (v. 1)—In general terms, this word means "one who is sent with a commission." The apostles of Jesus Christ—the Twelve and Paul—were special ambassadors or messengers chosen and trained by Christ to lay the foundation of

³ *Grace to you and peace from God the Father and our Lord Jesus Christ,*

⁴ *who gave Himself for our sins, that He might deliver us from this present evil age, according to the will of our God and Father,*

⁵ *to whom be glory forever and ever. Amen.*

⁶ *I marvel that you are turning away so soon from Him who called you in the grace of Christ, to a different gospel,*

⁷ *which is not another; but there are some who trouble you and want to pervert the gospel of Christ.*

⁸ *But even if we, or an angel from heaven, preach any other gospel to you than what we have preached to you, let him be accursed.*

⁹ *As we have said before, so now I say again, if anyone preaches any other gospel to you than what you have received, let him be accursed.*

the early church and be the channels of God's completed revelation (Ephesians 2:20).

not from men . . . but through Jesus Christ (v. 1)—To defend his apostleship against the false teachers' attack, Paul emphasized that Christ Himself had appointed him as an apostle before he met the other apostles (see vv. 17–18; Acts 9:3–9).

raised Him from the dead (v. 1)—Paul included this important fact to show that the risen and ascended Christ Himself had appointed him; thus Paul was a qualified witness of Christ's resurrection (see Acts 1:22).

churches of Galatia (v. 2)—the churches Paul founded at Antioch of Pisidia, Iconium, Lystra, and Derbe during his first missionary journey (Acts 13:14—14:23)

Grace to you and peace (v. 3)—Even Paul's typical greeting attacked the Judaizers' legalistic system; if salvation is by works as they claimed, it is not of "grace" and cannot result in "peace," since no one can be sure he or she has enough good works to be eternally secure.

for our sins (v. 4)—No one can avoid sin by human effort or law-keeping (Romans 3:20); therefore it must be forgiven, which Christ accomplished through His atoning death on the cross (Galatians 3:13).

present evil age (v. 4)—The Greek word for "age" does not refer to a period of time but an order or system and, in particular, to the current world system ruled by Satan (Romans 12:2; 1 John 2:15–16; 5:19).

the will of our God (v. 4)—The sacrifice of Christ for salvation was the will of God designed and fulfilled for His glory (see Matthew 26:42; John 6:38–40).

turning away (v. 6)—This is better

translated "deserting." The Greek word was used of military desertion which was punishable by death. The form of this Greek verb indicates that the Galatian believers were voluntarily deserting grace to pursue the legalism taught by the false teachers.

so soon (v. 6)—This Greek word can mean either "easily" or "quickly" and sometimes both. No doubt both senses characterized the Galatians' response to the false teachers' heretical doctrines.

called you (v. 6)—This could be translated "who called you once and for all" and refers to God's effectual call to salvation.

grace of Christ (v. 6)—God's free and sovereign act of mercy in granting salvation through the death and resurrection of Christ, totally apart from any human work or merit

different gospel (v. 6)—the Judaizers' perversion of the true gospel; They added the requirements, ceremonies, and standards of the Old Covenant as necessary prerequisites to salvation.

trouble (v. 7)—The Greek word could be translated "disturb" and means "to shake back and forth," meaning to agitate or stir up. Here it refers to the deep emotional disturbance that the Galatian believers experienced.

pervert (v. 7)—to turn something into its opposite. By adding law to the gospel of Christ, the false teachers were effectively destroying grace, turning the message of God's undeserved favor toward sinners into a message of earned and merited favor.

the gospel of Christ (v. 7)—the good news of salvation by grace alone through faith alone in Christ alone (Romans 1:1; 1 Corinthians 15:1–4)

we, or an angel from heaven (v. 8)—Paul's point is hypothetical, calling on the most unlikely examples for false teaching—himself and holy angels. The Galatians should receive no messenger, regardless of how impeccable his credentials, if his doctrine of salvation differs in the slightest degree from God's truth revealed through Christ and the apostles.

let him be accursed (v. 8)—The translation of this Greek word refers to devoting someone to destruction in eternal hell (see Romans 9:3; 1 Corinthians 12:3; 16:22). Throughout history, God has devoted certain objects, individuals, and groups of people to destruction (see Joshua 6:17–18; 7:1, 25–26). The New Testament offers many examples of one such group: false teachers (see Matthew 24:24; John 8:44; 1 Timothy 1:20; Titus 1:16). Here the Judaizers are identified as members of this infamous company.

As we have said before (v. 9)—This refers to what Paul taught during an earlier visit to these churches, not to a previous comment in this epistle.

anyone (v. 9)—Paul turns from the hypothetical case of verse 8 (the apostle or heavenly angels preaching a false gospel) to the real situation faced by the Galatians. The Judaizers were doing just that and were to be devoted to destruction because of their damning heresy.

Understanding the Text

3) How did Paul defend his apostleship? What was his primary argument?

_____

_____

_____

_____

_____

(verses to consider: Acts 9:1–15)

4) What was Paul's history with "the churches of Galatia"?

_____

_____

_____

_____

(verses to consider: Acts 13:14—14:23)

5) According to Paul, what is the only real solution for our sins?

_____

_____

_____

(verses to consider: Galatians 2:16; 3:19; Ephesians 2:8–9)

6) What did the death of Christ have to do with the will of God?

_____

_____

_____

_____

(verses to consider: Acts 2:22–23; Romans 8:3–4, 31–32; Ephesians 1:7, 11; Hebrews 10:4–10)

Cross-Reference

Read Romans 3:19–28:

¹⁹ *Now we know that whatever the law says, it says to those who are under the law, that every mouth may be stopped, and all the world may become guilty before God.*

²⁰ *Therefore by the deeds of the law no flesh will be justified in His sight, for by the law is the knowledge of sin.*

²¹ *But now the righteousness of God apart from the law is revealed, being witnessed by the Law and the Prophets,*

²² *even the righteousness of God, through faith in Jesus Christ, to all and on all who believe. For there is no difference;*

²³ *for all have sinned and fall short of the glory of God,*

²⁴ *being justified freely by His grace through the redemption that is in Christ Jesus,*

²⁵ *whom God set forth as a propitiation by His blood, through faith, to demonstrate His righteousness, because in His forbearance God had passed over the sins that were previously committed,*

²⁶ *to demonstrate at the present time His righteousness, that He might be just and the justifier of the one who has faith in Jesus.*

²⁷ *Where is boasting then? It is excluded. By what law? Of works? No, but by the law of faith.*

²⁸ *Therefore we conclude that a man is justified by faith apart from the deeds of the law.*

7) How does the Romans 3 passage address the exact problem the believers in Galatia were facing?

_____

_____

_____

_____

Exploring the Meaning

8) Read 2 Thessalonians 2:13–14. What does this say about the "call of God"? Why is this concept important for those who are tempted to turn away from grace and trust in works?

_____

_____

_____

_____

(verses to consider: 2 Timothy 1:8–9)

9) Read 2 Corinthians 11:4. What did Paul mean by a "different gospel"?

_____

_____

_____

_____

(verses to consider: Galatians 3:3; 4:9; Philippians 3:2)

Summing Up...

"The most destructive dangers to the church have never been atheism, pagan religions, or cults that openly deny Scripture, but rather supposedly Christian movements that accept so much biblical truth that their unscriptural doctrines seem relatively insignificant and harmless. But a single drop of poison in a large container can make all the water lethal. And a single false idea that in any way undercuts God's grace poisons the whole system of belief."
—*John MacArthur*

Reflecting on the Text

10) What is the simple gospel? Why is it such a hard message for so many to accept?

_____

_____

_____

11) Why do you think Paul reacted so harshly to the message of the Judaizers?

_____

_____

_____

_____

12) What is the danger of mixing grace with works?

_____

_____

_____

_____

13) List some relatives, friends, or neighbors who need to understand (and embrace) the gospel of grace. Pray for them this week, asking God for the opportunity to speak with them about the good news of forgiveness and freedom in Christ.

_____

_____

_____

_____

Recording Your Thoughts

_____

_____

_____

For further study, see the following verses:

Acts 1:2; 2:42   Romans 1:1, 4, 7; 3:24   2 Corinthians 5:19–21
Titus 3:4–5   1 Peter 2:24

Defending the Gospel

Opening Thought

1) What are some of your credentials (for example, heritage, training, experience)?

_____

_____

2) How have these factors combined to make you the person you are today?

_____

_____

3) In what ways are credentials important? To what degree and in what settings are they irrelevant?

_____

_____

4) How much of your motivation in life has to do with pleasing people? Why do you think this is so?

_____

_____

5) What is something that you do today about which you once said, "I would never do that!"?

_____

_____

Background of the Passage

After establishing churches in the region of Galatia on his first missionary journey, Paul learned that his work there was being undermined by a group commonly identified as the Judaizers. These Jewish loyalists were fiercely devoted to Mosaic ceremonies, standards, and practices and felt that Paul's gospel message was too far removed from its Jewish roots. They also argued that Paul's teaching was too easy and did not properly require enough demands of its adherents.

The Judaizers' response to this troublemaker named Paul was to try and thoroughly discredit him by attacking his credentials as an "apostle" of Christ. The strategy worked. Some Galatian believers began to question Paul's authority and legitimacy. Furthermore they questioned his motives. Most important, they began to doubt his message.

For all those reasons, Paul set out to defend his apostleship (1:10—2:10), explaining that he had been appointed by God and not by human beings. He offered a brief biographical sketch of important events in his life to further defend his calling and prove the authenticity of the gospel of grace he proclaimed. Then by recounting the details of his most significant trip to Jerusalem after his conversion, Paul offered convincing evidence that the message he proclaimed was identical to that of the other twelve apostles. By his coming, his companions, his commission, and his commendation, Paul powerfully demonstrated that he was of one truth and one spirit with the other twelve apostles. His gospel was independent in terms of revelation but identical in terms of content.

Paul's concern was not his own popularity or personal success but God's truth. At stake was the very integrity of the gospel.

Bible Passage

Read 1:10—2:10, noting the key words and definitions to the right of the passage.

Galatians 1:10—2:10

¹⁰ *For do I now persuade men, or God? Or do I seek to please men? For if I still pleased men, I would not be a bondservant of Christ.*

still pleased men (v. 10)—Paul's previous motivation when he used to persecute Christians on behalf of his fellow Jews

a bondservant of Christ (v. 10)—Paul had become a

11 But I make known to you, brethren, that the gospel which was preached by me is not according to man.

12 For I neither received it from man, nor was I taught it, but it came through the revelation of Jesus Christ.

13 For you have heard of my former conduct in Judaism, how I persecuted the church of God beyond measure and tried to destroy it.

14 And I advanced in Judaism beyond many of my contemporaries in my own nation, being more exceedingly zealous for the traditions of my fathers.

15 But when it pleased God, who separated me from my mother's womb and called me through His grace,

16 to reveal His Son in me, that I might preach Him among the Gentiles, I did not immediately confer with flesh and blood,

17 nor did I go up to Jerusalem to those who were apostles before me; but I went to Arabia, and returned again to Damascus.

18 Then after three years I went up to Jerusalem to see Peter, and remained with him fifteen days.

19 But I saw none of the other apostles except James, the Lord's brother.

20 (Now concerning the things which I write to you, indeed, before God, I do not lie.)

21 Afterward I went into the regions of Syria and Cilicia.

22 And I was unknown by face to the churches of Judea which were in Christ.

23 But they were hearing only, "He who formerly persecuted us now preaches the faith which he once tried to destroy."

24 And they glorified God in me.

2:1 Then after fourteen years I went up again to Jerusalem with Barnabas, and also took Titus with me.

willing slave of Christ, which cost him a great deal of suffering from others (6:17). Such personal sacrifice is exactly opposite the goal of pleasing men (6:12).

make known to you (v. 11)—The strong Greek verb used here would often introduce an important and emphatic statement (see 1 Corinthians 12:3).

the gospel . . . not according to man (v. 11)—The gospel Paul preached was not human in origin or it would have been like all other human religion, permeated with works righteousness born of human pride and Satan's deception.

neither received it from man, nor was I taught it (v. 12)—This is in contrast to the Judaizers, who received their religious instruction from rabbinic tradition. Most Jews did not study the actual Scriptures; instead, they used human interpretations of Scripture as their religious authority and guide. Many of their traditions were not only not taught in Scripture but also contradicted it.

through the revelation (v. 12)—This refers to the unveiling of something previously kept secret—in this case, Jesus Christ. While he knew about Christ, Paul subsequently met Him personally on the road to Damascus and received the truth of the gospel from Him (Acts 9:1–16).

Judaism (v. 13)—the Jewish religious system of works righteousness, based not primarily on the Old Testament text but on rabbinic interpretations and traditions; in fact, Paul will argue that a proper understanding of the Old Testament can lead only to Christ and His gospel of grace through faith (Galatians 3:6–29)

² *And I went up by revelation, and communicated to them that gospel which I preach among the Gentiles, but privately to those who were of reputation, lest by any means I might run, or had run, in vain.*

³ *Yet not even Titus who was with me, being a Greek, was compelled to be circumcised.*

⁴ *And this occurred because of false brethren secretly brought in (who came in by stealth to spy out our liberty which we have in Christ Jesus, that they might bring us into bondage),*

⁵ *to whom we did not yield submission even for an hour, that the truth of the gospel might continue with you.*

⁶ *But from those who seemed to be something— whatever they were, it makes no difference to me; God shows personal favoritism to no man—for those who seemed to be something added nothing to me.*

⁷ *But on the contrary, when they saw that the gospel for the uncircumcised had been committed to me, as the gospel for the circumcised was to Peter*

⁸ *(for He who worked effectively in Peter for the apostleship to the circumcised also worked effectively in me toward the Gentiles),*

⁹ *and when James, Cephas, and John, who seemed to be pillars, perceived the grace that had been given to me, they gave me and Barnabas the right hand of fellowship, that we should go to the Gentiles and they to the circumcised.*

¹⁰ *They desired only that we should remember the poor, the very thing which I also was eager to do.*

persecuted (v. 13)—The tense of this Greek verb emphasizes Paul's persistent and continual effort to hurt and ultimately exterminate Christians.

advanced . . . beyond (v. 14) — The Greek word for "advanced" means "to chop ahead," much like one would blaze a trail through a forest. Paul blazed his path in Judaism (see Philippians 3:5–6), and because he saw Jewish Christians as obstacles to its advancement, he worked to cut them down.

exceedingly zealous (v. 14)— Paul demonstrated this by the extent to which he pursued and persecuted Christians.

traditions of my fathers (v. 14) —the oral teachings about Old Testament law commonly known as the "Halakah." This collection of interpretations of the law eventually carried the same authority as, or even greater than, the law (Torah) itself; its regulations were so hopelessly complex and burdensome that even the most astute rabbinical scholars could not master it by either interpretation or conduct.

separated me from my mother's womb (v. 15)—Paul is not talking about being born, separated physically from his mother but being separated or set apart to God for service from the time of his birth. The phrase refers to God's election of Paul without regard for his personal merit or effort (see Isaiah 49:1).

called me through His grace (v. 15)—This refers to God's effectual call. On the Damascus Road God actually brought Saul, whom He had already chosen, to salvation.

reveal His Son in me (v. 16)— Not only was Christ revealed to Paul on the Damascus Road, but in him as God gave him the life, light, and faith to believe in Him.

preach Him among the Gentiles (v. 16)—Paul's specific call to proclaim the gospel to non-Jews

confer with flesh and blood (v. 16)—Paul did not look to Ananias or other Christians at Damascus for clarification of or addition to the revelation he received from Christ (Acts 9:19–20).

Jerusalem . . . Arabia . . . Damascus (v. 17)—Rather than immediately travel to Jerusalem to be instructed by the apostles, Paul instead went to Nabatean Arabia, a wilderness that stretched east of Damascus down to the Sinai peninsula. After being prepared for ministry by the Lord, he returned to minister in nearby Damascus.

three years (v. 18)—the approximate time from Paul's conversion to his first journey to Jerusalem. During those years he made a visit to Damascus and resided in Arabia, under the instruction of the Lord; this visit is discussed in Acts 9:26–30.

up to Jerusalem (v. 18)—Travelers in Israel always speak of going up to Jerusalem because of its higher elevation.

see (v. 18)—better translated "to become acquainted with"

Peter (v. 18)—the apostle who was the personal companion of the Lord and the most powerful spokesman in the early years of the Jerusalem church (Acts 1–12)

I do not lie (v. 20)—The directness of this statement indicates that Paul had been accused by the Jewish legalists of being a liar who was shameless or deluded.

Syria and Cilicia (v. 21)—This area included Paul's hometown of Tarsus—he preached in that region for several years. When word of revival in that area reached Jerusalem, they sent Barnabas (see Acts 11:20–26). Paul stayed in that region as a pastor in the church at Antioch. Then, with Barnabas, he went from there on the first missionary journey (Acts 13:1–3) and, afterward, returned to Antioch (Acts 13:1–3). From there they were sent to the Jerusalem Council (Acts 14:26—15:4).

fourteen years . . . again to Jerusalem (2:1)—This was the period from the time of his first visit to Jerusalem (Gal. 1:18) to the one to which Paul refers here, which probably was for the Jerusalem Council (Acts 15:1–22) called to resolve the issue of Gentile salvation. Linguistically, the word "again" need not refer to the next visit; it can just as easily mean "once again" without respect to how many visits took place in between. Paul did, in fact, visit Jerusalem during that fourteen-year period to deliver famine relief to the church there (Acts 11:27–30; 12:24–25), but he does not refer to that visit here since it had no bearing on his apostolic authority.

Barnabas (v.1)—Paul's first ally who vouched for him before the apostles at Jerusalem (Acts 9:27) and who became Paul's traveling companion on his first missionary journey (Acts 13:2–3)

Titus (v. 1)—a spiritual child of Paul and a coworker (Titus 1:4–5); as an uncircumcised Gentile, Titus was fitting proof of the effectiveness of Paul's ministry.

by revelation (v. 2)—This revelation from God was the voice of the Holy Spirit. Paul referred to the divine commissioning of his visit in order to refute any suggestion by the Judaizers that they had sent Paul to Jerusalem to have the apostles correct his doctrine.

those who were of reputation (v. 2)—the three main leaders of the Jerusalem church: Peter, James (the Lord's brother, 1:19), and John (see verse 9). This phrase was typically used of authorities and implied a position of honor. Paul referred to them in a similar way two other times (verses 6, 9), suggesting a hint of sarcasm directed toward the Judaizers, who claimed they had apostolic approval for their doctrine and Paul did not; they had likely made a habit of exalting these three leaders at Paul's expense.

might run . . . in vain (v. 2)—Paul hoped the Jerusalem leaders would support his ministry to the Gentiles and not soften their opposition to legalism. He did not want to see his ministry efforts wasted because of conflict with the other apostles.

compelled to be circumcised (v. 3)—At the core of the Judaizers' works system was the Mosaic prescription of circumcision. They were teaching that there could be no salvation without circumcision (Acts 15:1, 5, 24). Paul and the apostles denied that assertion, and it was settled at the Jerusalem Council. As a true believer, Titus was living proof that circumcision and the Mosaic regulations were not prerequisites or necessary components of salvation. The apostles' refusal to require Titus' circumcision verified the church's rejection of the Judaizers' doctrine.

false brethren (v. 4)—the Judaizers, who pretended to be true Christians; yet their doctrine, because it claimed allegiance to Christ, was opposed to traditional Judaism, and, because it demanded circumcision and obedience to the Mosaic law as prerequisites for salvation, was opposed to Christianity.

to spy out (v. 4)—The Greek word pictures spies or traitors entering by stealth into an enemy's camp. The Judaizers were Satan's undercover agents sent into the midst of the church to sabotage the true gospel.

liberty (v. 4)—Christians are free from the law as a means of salvation, from its external ceremonial regulations as a way of living and from its curse for disobedience to the law—a curse that Christ bore for all believers (3:13). This freedom is not, however, a license to sin (5:13).

bondage (v. 4)—conveys the idea of absolute slavery to an impossible system of works righteousness

those who seemed to be something (v. 6)—another reference to Peter, James, and John

personal favoritism (v. 6)—The unique privileges of the Twelve did not make their apostleship more legitimate or authoritative than Paul's—Christ commissioned them all (see Romans 2:11). Paul never saw himself as apostolically inferior.

for the uncircumcised (v.7)—better translated "to the uncircumcised"; Paul preached the gospel primarily to the Gentiles (also to Jews in Gentile lands, as his pattern was to go to the synagogue first; see Acts 13:5).

circumcised . . . Peter (v.7)—Peter's ministry was primarily to the Jews.

He who worked effectively in Peter . . . in me (v. 8)—The Holy Spirit, who has but one gospel, empowered both Peter and Paul in their ministries.

pillars (v. 9)—emphasizing the role of James, Peter, and John in establishing and supporting the church

the right hand of fellowship (v. 9)—In the Near East, this represented a solemn vow of friendship and a mark of partnership. This act signified the apostles' recognition of Paul as a teacher of the true gospel and a partner in ministry.

remember the poor (v. 10)—a practical reminder for Paul and the growing ranks of Gentile Christians; the number of Christians in Jerusalem grew rapidly at first (see Acts 2:41–45; 6:1), and many who were visiting the city for the feast of Pentecost (Acts 2:1, 5) remained and never returned to their homes; while the believers initially shared their resources (Acts 2:45; 4:32–37), many had little money, and for years the Jerusalem church was economically pressed.

Understanding the Text

6) What does Paul reveal here about himself in the area of people-pleasing?

_____

_____

_____

_____

_____

_____

7) Why did Paul bother to recount his prior acts of persecution against believers?

_____

_____

_____

_____

_____

_____

(verses to consider: Acts 8:1–3; 9:1–2; 1 Timothy 1:12–16)

8) How does Paul's dramatic conversion demonstrate the truth of election?

_____

_____

_____

_____

(verses to consider: Jeremiah 1:5; Romans 9:10–23)

9) Why was Paul's ministry to Gentiles so offensive to the Jews?

_____

_____

_____

_____

_____

_____

(verses to consider: Acts 26:15–18; Romans 1:13–16)

Cross-Reference

Read Philippians 3:1–14:

¹ *Finally, my brethren, rejoice in the Lord. For me to write the same things to you is not tedious, but for you it is safe.*

² *Beware of dogs, beware of evil workers, beware of the mutilation!*

³ *For we are the circumcision, who worship God in the Spirit, rejoice in Christ Jesus, and have no confidence in the flesh,*

⁴ *though I also might have confidence in the flesh. If anyone else thinks he may have confidence in the flesh, I more so:*

⁵ *circumcised the eighth day, of the stock of Israel, of the tribe of Benjamin, a Hebrew of the Hebrews; concerning the law, a Pharisee;*

⁶ *concerning zeal, persecuting the church; concerning the righteousness which is in the law, blameless.*

⁷ *But what things were gain to me, these I have counted loss for Christ.*

⁸ *Yet indeed I also count all things loss for the excellence of the knowledge of Christ Jesus my Lord, for whom I have suffered the loss of all things, and count them as rubbish, that I may gain Christ*

⁹ *and be found in Him, not having my own righteousness, which is from the law, but that which is through faith in Christ, the righteousness which is from God by faith;*

¹⁰ *that I may know Him and the power of His resurrection, and the fellowship of His sufferings, being conformed to His death,*

¹¹ *if, by any means, I may attain to the resurrection from the dead.*

¹² Not that I have already attained, or am already perfected; but I press on, that I may lay hold of that for which Christ Jesus has also laid hold of me.

¹³ Brethren, I do not count myself to have apprehended; but one thing I do, forgetting those things which are behind and reaching forward to those things which are ahead,

¹⁴ I press toward the goal for the prize of the upward call of God in Christ Jesus.

10) How does Paul's testimony in Philippians 3 corroborate his statements in 1:10—2:10?

_____

_____

_____

_____

_____

_____

_____

_____

Exploring the Meaning

11) Read Genesis 17:9–14. What was the point of circumcision for the Jews?

_____

_____

_____

_____

_____

_____

(verses to consider: Romans 4:9–12)

12) Read Acts 15:1–22. How did the events and decisions of the Jerusalem Council give credence to Paul's apostolic claims?

_____

_____

_____

_____

_____

Summing Up...

"No human explanation or influence could account for the 180 degree turn-around in Saul's life. He had been like a runaway freight train that crushes everything in its path. He had lost control of his life and was without restraint. His legalistic zeal had put him on a headlong course of destruction from which no natural force short of death could have deterred him. His apostolic calling could only have been supernatural and sovereign, completely apart from human testimony or persuasion (though he may have heard much truth from the Christians he captured)." —*John MacArthur*

Reflecting on the Text

13) If a group of religious people attacked your character and motives and accused you of propagating a suspect faith, how would you answer them? What evidence would you marshal to establish your authenticity as a servant of the Lord Jesus Christ?

_____

_____

_____

_____

_____

_____

_____

_____

14) The chances are pretty good that your pastor is facing unfair criticism today. (Most ministers are under a pretty steady barrage of untrue accusations and unwarranted attacks.) How could you (concretely and practically) offer encouragement to your pastor today?

_____

_____

_____

_____

_____

_____

15) Which of your credentials ultimately matters the most? How can you better use your gifts, experiences, and training to serve the Lord more effectively this week?

_____

_____

_____

_____

_____

_____

_____

_____

Recording Your Thoughts

_____

_____

_____

_____

_____

_____

_____

_____

_____

_____

_____

_____

_____

_____

_____

_____

_____

_____

_____

_____

_____

For further study, see the following verses:

Matthew 10:2   Mark 7:13   Acts 4:36; 13:2–4; 15:13

Acts 16:1–3; 18:22; 26:11   Romans 1:1, 14, 16; 8:30   2 Corinthians 8:1

2 Corinthians 12:11–12

Crucified with Christ

Galatians 2:11–21

Opening Thought

1) How do you react when you see someone doing something that is clearly wrong? That is, on a scale of 1–10 (with 1 representing "immediate confrontation" and 10 symbolizing "live and let live") what is your typical response? Why?

#2

_____

_____

_____

2) How much does our society's emphasis on tolerance contribute to the rarity of confronting others with truth?

Great extent

_____

_____

_____

3) What is it about human nature that balks at the notion of grace?

Grace is God's righteous

_____

_____

_____

_____

Background of the Passage

Early Christianity had a distinctivly Jewish flavor. The early church began almost exclusively with converts from Jewish backgrounds and personal histories steeped in Hebrew traditions and practices. When large numbers of Gentiles also began embracing Jesus Christ as Messiah, the result was a collision of very radically different cultural and religious worlds.

In and around this strange and new entity called the church rose a group determined to cling to the old legalism of the Mosaic law. These were the Judaizers—devout God-fearing people claiming to follow Christ but teaching that Gentiles must be circumcised and adhere to the Mosaic law in order to be saved. It was, so they claimed, necessary to keep the law in order to maintain a right relationship with God.

Not only did these Judaizers distort the gospel and confuse the Gentile converts in Galatia, but they also called into question Paul's apostolic claims. In response, Paul wrote Galatians, a very stern and blunt letter about the good news of justification by faith.

In 2:11–21, Paul told of the time that he had to confront Peter, the preeminent apostle, because of Peter's failure to live up to the truth of the gospel. Peter had withdrawn from the Gentile believers to fellowship with the Judaizers, although they held a position he knew was wrong. By so doing, Peter had in appearance supported their doctrine and had nullified Paul's divine teaching, especially the doctrine of salvation by grace alone through faith alone. Paul's rebuke of Peter serves as one of the most dynamic statements in the New Testament on the absolute and unwavering necessity of the doctrine of justification by grace through faith. Peter's apparent repentance acknowledged Paul's apostolic authority and his own submission to the truth (see 2 Peter 3:15, 16).

Bible Passage

Read 2:11–21, noting the key words and definitions to the right of the passage.

Galatians 2:11–21

11 Now when Peter had come to Antioch, I withstood him to his face, because he was to be blamed;

Antioch (v. 11)—the location of the first Gentile church

to be blamed (v. 11)—better translated "stood condemned";

¹² *for before certain men came from James, he would eat with the Gentiles; but when they came, he withdrew and separated himself, fearing those who were of the circumcision.*

¹³ *And the rest of the Jews also played the hypocrite with him, so that even Barnabas was carried away with their hypocrisy.*

¹⁴ *But when I saw that they were not straightforward about the truth of the gospel, I said to Peter before them all, "If you, being a Jew, live in the manner of Gentiles and not as the Jews, why do you compel Gentiles to live as Jews?*

¹⁵ *We who are Jews by nature, and not sinners of the Gentiles,*

¹⁶ *knowing that a man is not justified by the works of the law but by faith in Jesus Christ, even we have believed in Christ Jesus, that we might be justified by faith in Christ and not by the works of the law; for by the works of the law no flesh shall be justified.*

¹⁷ *But if, while we seek to be justified by Christ, we ourselves also are found sinners, is Christ therefore a minister of sin? Certainly not!*

¹⁸ *For if I build again those things which I destroyed, I make myself a transgressor.*

¹⁹ *For I through the law died to the law that I might live to God.*

²⁰ *I have been crucified with Christ; it is no longer I who live, but Christ lives in me; and the life which I now live in the flesh I live by faith in the Son of God, who loved me and gave Himself for me.*

²¹ *I do not set aside the grace of God; for if righteousness comes through the law, then Christ died in vain."*

Peter was guilty of sin by aligning himself with men he knew to be in error and because of the harm and confusion he caused his Gentile brethren.

certain men . . . from James (v. 12)—Peter, knowing the decision the Jerusalem Council had made (Acts 15:7–29), had been in Antioch for some time, eating with Gentiles. When Judaizers came, pretending to be sent by James, they lied, giving false claims of support from the apostles. Peter had already given up all Mosaic ceremony (Acts 10:9–22), and James had, at times, held only to some of it (Acts 21:18–26).

withdrew (v. 12)—The Greek term refers to strategic military withdrawal. The verb's form may imply that Peter's withdrawal was gradual and deceptive. To eat with the Judaizers and decline invitations to eat with the Gentiles, which he had previously done, meant that Peter was affirming the very dietary restrictions he knew God had abolished (Acts 10:15) and thus striking a blow at the gospel of grace.

fearing those . . . of the circumcision (v. 12)—The true motivation behind Peter's defection was that he was afraid of losing popularity with the legalistic, Judaizing segment of people in the church, even though they were self-righteous hypocrites promoting a heretical doctrine.

the rest of the Jews (v. 13)—the Jewish believers in Antioch

hypocrite (v. 13)—This Greek word refers to an actor who would wear a mask to depict a mood or certain character. In the spiritual sense, it refers to someone who masks his true character by pretending to be something he is not—they were committed to the gospel of grace but were pretending to accept Jewish legalism.

straightforward (v. 14)—literally, to walk "straight" or "uprightly." By withdrawing from the Gentile Christians, Peter and the other Jewish believers were not walking in line with God's Word.

live in the manner of Gentiles (v. 14)—Before his gradual withdrawal, Peter regularly had fellowship and ate with the Gentiles, thus modeling the ideal of Christian love and liberty between Jew and Gentile.

compel Gentiles to live as Jews (v. 14)—By his Judaizing mandate, Peter was declaring that theirs was the right way.

sinners of the Gentiles (v. 15)—This is used in the legal sense since Gentiles were sinners by nature because they had no revealed, divine, written law to guide them toward salvation or living righteously.

works . . . faith (v. 16)—Three times this verse declares that salvation is only through faith in Christ and not by law. The first is general, "a man is not justified"; the second is personal, "we might be justified"; and the third is universal, "no flesh shall be justified."

justified (v. 16)—This basic forensic Greek word describes a judge declaring an accused person not guilty and therefore innocent before the law. Throughout Scripture it refers to God's declaring a sinner not guilty and fully righteous before Him by imputing to him the divine righteousness of Christ and imputing the person's sin to the sinless Savior for punishment.

works of the law (v. 16)—Keeping the law is not a means of salvation because the root of sinfulness is in the fallenness of a person's heart, not his or her actions. The law served as a mirror to reveal sin, not a cure for it.

we . . . are found sinners (v. 17)—If the Judaizers' doctrine was correct, then Paul, Peter, Barnabas, and the other Jewish believers had fallen back into the category of sinners because they had been eating and fellowshiping with Gentiles, who, according to the Judaizers, were unclean.

minister of sin (v. 17)—If the Judaizers were right, then Christ was wrong and had been teaching people to sin because He taught that food could not contaminate a person. Jesus also had declared that all who belong to Him are one with Him and therefore each other (John 17:21–23). Paul's airtight logic condemned Peter because by his actions he had, in effect, made it appear as if Christ were lying. This thought is utterly objectionable and caused Paul to use the strongest Greek negative ("certainly not"; see 3:21; Romans 6:1–2; 7:13).

things which I destroyed (v. 18)—the false system of salvation through legalism, done away with by the preaching of salvation by grace alone through faith alone

died to the law (v. 19)—When a person is convicted of a capital crime and executed, the law has no further claim on that person. So it is with the Christian who has died in Christ (who paid the penalty for his sins in full) and rises to new life in Him—justice has been satisfied and the believer is forever free from any further penalty.

I have been crucified with Christ (v. 20)—A person who trusts in Christ for salvation spiritually participates with the Lord in His crucifixion and victory over sin and death.

no longer I who live, but Christ lives in me (v. 20)—The believer's old self is dead, having been crucified with Christ (Romans 6:3, 5). The believer's new person has the privilege of the indwelling Christ empowering him or her and living through him or her.

gave Himself for me (v. 20)—the manifestation of Christ's love for the believer through His sacrificial death on the cross

Christ died in vain (v. 21)—This can be better translated, "Christ died needlessly." Those who insist that they can earn salvation by their own efforts undermine the foundation of Christianity and render unnecessary the death of Christ.

Understanding the Text

4) How did Peter deviate from the true gospel and become hypocritical? How did Paul respond?

Eating w/ G

Paul's R7-4l

(verses to consider: Acts 10)

5) If the law is incapable of saving people, as Paul argued, what is the law's purpose?

to be us to Christ

(verses to consider: Romans 7:7–13:1; Galatians 3:22–25; 1 Timothy 1:8–11)

6) How did Paul contrast the teaching of the Judaizers with the teaching of Christ?

The law vs. Christs love

_____

_____

_____

(verses to consider: Mark 7:18–23; John 17:20–23; Acts 10:13–15)

7) According to 2:20–21, how does the believer's union with Christ refute the argument of the Judaizers and the wrong behavior of Peter?

_____ 1 ᵩ _____

_____

_____

_____

_____

Cross-Reference

Read Acts 11:1–18:

¹ *Now the apostles and brethren who were in Judea heard that the Gentiles had also received the word of God.*

² *And when Peter came up to Jerusalem, those of the circumcision contended with him,*

³ *saying, "You went in to uncircumcised men and ate with them!"*

⁴ *But Peter explained it to them in order from the beginning, saying:*

⁵ *"I was in the city of Joppa praying; and in a trance I saw a vision, an object descending like a great sheet, let down from heaven by four corners; and it came to me.*

⁶ *When I observed it intently and considered, I saw four-footed animals of the earth, wild beasts, creeping things, and birds of the air.*

⁷ *And I heard a voice saying to me, 'Rise, Peter; kill and eat.'*

⁸ *But I said, 'Not so, Lord! For nothing common or unclean has at any time entered my mouth.'*

⁹ *But the voice answered me again from heaven, 'What God has cleansed you must not call common.'*

10 *Now this was done three times, and all were drawn up again into heaven.*

11 *At that very moment, three men stood before the house where I was, having been sent to me from Caesarea.*

12 *Then the Spirit told me to go with them, doubting nothing. Moreover these six brethren accompanied me, and we entered the man's house.*

13 *And he told us how he had seen an angel standing in his house, who said to him, 'Send men to Joppa, and call for Simon whose surname is Peter,*

14 *who will tell you words by which you and all your household will be saved.'*

15 *And as I began to speak, the Holy Spirit fell upon them, as upon us at the beginning.*

16 *Then I remembered the word of the Lord, how He said, 'John indeed baptized with water, but you shall be baptized with the Holy Spirit.'*

17 *If therefore God gave them the same gift as He gave us when we believed on the Lord Jesus Christ, who was I that I could withstand God?"*

18 *When they heard these things they became silent; and they glorified God, saying, "Then God has also granted to the Gentiles repentance to life."*

8) According to this passage, what did Christ teach Peter through his encounter with Cornelius?

_____

_____

_____

_____

_____

_____

Exploring the Meaning

9) Read Romans 6:2–6. How does this passage amplify Paul's statement in 2:20?

_____

_____

_____

_____

_____

_____

(verses to consider: Romans 8:9–10; Ephesians 4:22)

10) Read John 10:17. How did Christ demonstrate his love for believers? Why is it important not to take this truth for granted or to allow it to become old?

_____ b gv ʊ life) _____

_____

_____

_____

_____

(verses to consider: Romans 5:6–8)

Summing Up...

"The two pillars of the gospel are the grace of God and the death of Christ, and those are the two pillars that, by its very nature, legalism destroys. The person who insists that he can earn salvation by his own efforts undermines the very foundation of Christianity and nullifies the precious death of Christ on his behalf."—*John MacArthur*

Reflecting on the Text

11) The Galatian believers were tempted by the Judaizers to think that human effort in keeping Jewish laws and customs was essential to salvation. Modern-day Christians don't typically try to adhere to the Mosaic law in an attempt to earn God's favor, but what kinds of "Christian" laws are often held up as necessary for meeting God's approval?

11-19-03

12) Could you confront a Christian friend who was obviously straying from the truth? What is the key to confrontation that honors God?

[handwritten, illegible]

13) What truth or principle from this lesson has had the greatest impact on you personally? Why? What will you do differently as a result?

1 Peter 3:15 _[handwritten, illegible]_

Recording Your Thoughts

_____

_____

_____

_____

_____

_____

_____

_____

_____

_____

_____

_____

_____

_____

_____

_____

_____

_____

_____

For further study, see the following verses:

Matthew 6:1–6   Acts 11:19   Romans 1:17; 3:24
Philippians 3:8–9

Justification by Faith

Opening Thought

1) What is the most foolish thing you've either witnessed or heard about in the last few weeks?

Homo priest ordained

2) How would you define "foolishness"?

3) What happened to exasperate you recently?

Background of the Passage

Paul had been used by the Lord to introduce the gospel of sovereign grace to the Galatians, bringing them the truth that salvation is received through faith in Christ's atoning work on the cross plus nothing else. Now, due to the powerful influence of the Judaizers, these believers were drifting and had accepted an inferior and impotent substitute based on the old Mosaic rituals and ceremonial standards that the New Covenant in Christ had made invalid—and that, even under the Old Covenant, had no power to save.

The defecting believers had not lost their salvation, but they had lost the joy and freedom of it and had returned, deceived, to the uncertainty and bondage of a self-imposed legalism. They were still in Christ and right with God positionally, but they were not practically living in conformity to the truth by which they had been made righteous. Having substituted a form of religion, they had no power or joy for the fullness of life in Christ that they once enjoyed.

Because these believers had allowed themselves to be deceived, they also were projecting to the deceived unbelievers around them the thinking that Christianity was a matter of law rather than faith. They had robbed themselves of the fullness of God's blessing and were in danger of robbing the world of the knowledge of the only way of salvation.

In this lesson's passage, Paul reminds the Galatians that a believer's experience of the Lord Jesus Christ, of the Holy Spirit, and of God the Father is incontrovertible evidence of having been graciously made acceptable to God through personal faith in the perfect and complete work of Christ, apart from any human supplement. Paul uses Abraham as proof that salvation has never come any other way than by grace through faith. Even the Old Testament teaches justification by faith.

Bible Passage

Read 3:1–9, noting the key words and definitions to the right of the passage.

Galatians 3:1–9

¹ *O foolish Galatians! Who has bewitched you that you should not obey the truth, before whose eyes*

foolish (v. 1)—This refers not to lack of intelligence but to lack of obedience (see Luke 24:25; 1 Timothy 6:9). Paul expressed his shock, surprise, and outrage at the Galatians' defection.

Jesus Christ was clearly portrayed among you as crucified?

2 *This only I want to learn from you: Did you receive the Spirit by the works of the law, or by the hearing of faith?*

3 *Are you so foolish? Having begun in the Spirit, are you now being made perfect by the flesh?*

4 *Have you suffered so many things in vain—if indeed it was in vain?*

5 *Therefore He who supplies the Spirit to you and works miracles among you, does He do it by the works of the law, or by the hearing of faith?—*

6 *just as Abraham "believed God, and it was accounted to him for righteousness."*

7 *Therefore know that only those who are of faith are sons of Abraham.*

8 *And the Scripture, foreseeing that God would justify the Gentiles by faith, preached the gospel to Abraham beforehand, saying, "In you all the nations shall be blessed."*

9 *So then those who are of faith are blessed with believing Abraham.*

Who . . . ? (v. 1)—The Judaizers, the Jewish false teachers, were plaguing the Galatian churches.

bewitched (v. 1)—charmed or misled by flattery and false promises; the term suggests an appeal to the emotions

clearly portrayed (v. 1)—The Greek word describes the posting of official notices in public places. Paul's preaching had publicly displayed the true gospel of Jesus Christ before the Galatians.

crucified (v. 1)—The crucifixion of Christ was a one-time historical fact with continuing results into eternity. Christ's sacrificial death provides eternal payment for believers' sins (see Hebrews 7:25) and does not need to be supplemented by any human works.

Did you receive the Spirit. . . ? (v. 2)—The answer to Paul's rhetorical question is obvious; the Galatians had received the Spirit when they were saved (Romans 8:9; 1 John 3:24), not through keeping the law, but through saving faith granted when hearing the gospel (see Romans 10:17)—the hearing of faith is actually hearing with faith. Paul appealed to the Galatians' own salvation to refute the Judaizers' false teaching that keeping the law is necessary for salvation.

Are you so foolish? (v. 3)—Incredulous at how easily the Galatians had been duped, Paul asked a second rhetorical question, again rebuking them for their foolishness.

begun in the Spirit . . . by the flesh (v. 3)—The notion that sinful, weak, fallen human nature could improve on the saving work of the Holy Spirit was ludicrous to Paul.

suffered (v. 4)—The Greek word has the basic meaning of "experienced" and does not necessarily imply pain or hardship. Paul used it to describe the Galatians' personal experience of salvation in Jesus Christ.

many things (v. 4)—This refers to all the blessings of salvation from God, Christ, and the Holy Spirit (see Ephesians 1:3).

sons of Abraham (v. 7)—quoted from Genesis 15:6; believing Jews and Gentiles are the true spiritual children of Abraham because they follow his example of faith (see Galatians 3:29; Romans 4:11, 16).

Scripture, foreseeing (v. 8)—Personifying the Scriptures was a common Jewish figure of speech (see Gal. 4:30; John 7:38, 42; 19:37; Romans 9:17; 11:2). Because Scripture is God's Word, when it speaks, God speaks.

preached the gospel to Abraham (v. 8)—The "good news" to Abraham was the news of salvation for all the nations (quoted from Genesis 12:3; 18:18—see Genesis 22:18; John 8:56; Acts 26:22–23). Salvation has always been by faith.

those who are of faith . . . Abraham (v. 9)—whether Jew or Gentile; the Old Testament predicted that Gentiles would receive the blessings of justification by faith, as did Abraham; those blessings are poured out on all because of Christ (see John 1:16; Ephesians 1:3; Colossians 2:10; 2 Peter 1:3–4)

Understanding the Text

4) Why did Paul say that the Galatians were "foolish" and "bewitched"?

_____

_____

_____

_____

_____

(verses to consider: Luke 24:25; Romans 12:1, 2)

5) What does Paul say about the connection between the Holy Spirit and salvation? Specifically, when do believers receive the Spirit?

_____

_____

_____

_____

6) Why was Paul so agitated by the Judaizers' contention that fleshly effort was both needful and necessary?

_____

_____

_____

_____

_____

7) What does this passage say about spiritual blessings coming upon people (not just devout Jews) because of faith in Christ?

_____

_____

_____

_____

(verses to consider: Romans 8:32; Ephesians 2:6–7)

Cross-Reference

Read Romans 4:1–25:

¹ *What then shall we say that Abraham our father has found according to the flesh?*

² *For if Abraham was justified by works, he has something to boast about, but not before God.*

³ *For what does the Scripture say? "Abraham believed God, and it was accounted to him for righteousness."*

⁴ *Now to him who works, the wages are not counted as grace but as debt.*

⁵ *But to him who does not work but believes on Him who justifies the ungodly, his faith is accounted for righteousness,*

⁶ *just as David also describes the blessedness of the man to whom God imputes righteousness apart from works:*

⁷ *"Blessed are those whose lawless deeds are forgiven, and whose sins are covered;*

⁸ *Blessed is the man to whom the Lord shall not impute sin."*

⁹ *Does this blessedness then come upon the circumcised only, or upon the uncircumcised also? For we say that faith was accounted to Abraham for righteousness.*

¹⁰ *How then was it accounted? While he was circumcised, or uncircumcised? Not while circumcised, but while uncircumcised.*

¹¹ *And he received the sign of circumcision, a seal of the righteousness of the faith which he had while still uncircumcised, that he might be the father of all those who believe, though they are uncircumcised, that righteousness might be imputed to them also,*

¹² *and the father of circumcision to those who not only are of the circumcision, but who also walk in the steps of the faith which our father Abraham had while still uncircumcised.*

¹³ *For the promise that he would be the heir of the world was not to Abraham or to his seed through the law, but through the righteousness of faith.*

¹⁴ *For if those who are of the law are heirs, faith is made void and the promise made of no effect,*

¹⁵ *because the law brings about wrath; for where there is no law there is no transgression.*

¹⁶ *Therefore it is of faith that it might be according to grace, so that the promise might be sure to all the seed, not only to those who are of the law, but also to those who are of the faith of Abraham, who is the father of us all*

¹⁷ *(as it is written, "I have made you a father of many nations") in the presence of Him whom he believed—God, who gives life to the dead and calls those things which do not exist as though they did;*

¹⁸ *who, contrary to hope, in hope believed, so that he became the father of many nations, according to what was spoken, "So shall your descendants be."*

¹⁹ *And not being weak in faith, he did not consider his own body, already dead (since he was about a hundred years old), and the deadness of Sarah's womb.*

²⁰ *He did not waver at the promise of God through unbelief, but was strengthened in faith, giving glory to God,*

²¹ *and being fully convinced that what He had promised He was also able to perform.*

²² *And therefore "it was accounted to him for righteousness."*

²³ *Now it was not written for his sake alone that it was imputed to him,*

²⁴ *but also for us. It shall be imputed to us who believe in Him who raised up Jesus our Lord from the dead,*

²⁵ *who was delivered up because of our offenses, and was raised because of our justification.*

8) According to this passage what is the connection between circumcision (or any other religious ritual, for that matter) and salvation?

_____

_____

_____

_____

_____

_____

Exploring the Meaning

9) Read Romans 2:28–29. What does this passage say about circumcision? About "circumcision . . . of the heart"? What does this mean?

_____

_____

_____

_____

_____

_____

10) Read Ephesians 1:13–14. What light does this passage shed upon the timing of the indwelling of the Holy Spirit?

_____

_____

_____

_____

_____

_____

Summing Up...

"The validity of good works in God's sight depends on whose power they are done in and for whose glory. When they are done in the power of His Spirit and for His glory, they are beautiful and acceptable to Him. When they are done in the power of the flesh and for the sake of personal recognition or merit, they are rejected by Him. Legalism is separated from true obedience by attitude. The one is a rotten smell in God's nostrils, whereas the other is a sweet savor."—*John MacArthur*

Reflecting on the Text

11) Some believers fall prey to formalism, substituting external ceremonies and rites for the internal reality of personal growth in the Lord. Others fall into legalistic systems of dos and don'ts, proudly hoping to improve their standing before God by doing or not doing certain things. Still others look for a second blessing—a spiritual secret to unlock some higher plane of spiritual reality, hoping to receive more of God than they imagine was granted to them at conversion. To which of these errors are you most prone and why?

_____

_____

_____

_____

_____

_____

12) What commonly accepted rules have many Christians tried to make part of the gospel? How is this similar to what the Judaizers were doing among the Galatian believers?

_____

_____

_____

_____

_____

_____

13) What young Christians do you know who are struggling much as the Galatians did? How can you help them today break free from the bondage of trying to earn God's approval through human effort?

_____

_____

_____

_____

_____

_____

Recording Your Thoughts

_____

_____

_____

_____

_____

_____

_____

_____

_____

_____

_____

_____

_____

For further study, see the following verses:

Genesis 12:3; 15:6; 18:18

Luke 8:13

Acts 8:13, 21

Romans 4:3; 10:11

1 Corinthians 15:2

2 Corinthians 6:1

2 Corinthians 13:5–6

Ephesians 1:3

1 Timothy 5:18

Titus 3:3

The Law and the Promise

Galatians 3:10–18

Opening Thought

1) When was the last big argument you had? What was it all about? What happened?

_____

_____

_____

_____

2) In arguments what tactics do you typically resort to? Are you more cerebral or more emotional? How logical are you? Can you lay out a compelling case, or are you scattered in your thoughts?

_____

_____

_____

_____

3) If you had to make the case for grace to a religious friend who insisted that "salvation *can't* be a free gift! Surely, we *have* to do our part!" what would you say?

_____

_____

_____

_____

_____

Background of the Passage

Following the preaching of the gospel and the establishment of churches across Asia Minor on Paul's first missionary journey, a disturbing development occurred. A persuasive and influential group of Jewish legalists infiltrated the churches and insisted upon the necessity of following Jewish rites and traditions in order to experience salvation.

Paul saw this as nothing less than a devilish assault on the pure and simple gospel of justification by faith. So he wrote what we know as the Epistle to the Galatians, a stern letter of reproof and a wonderful exposition of how Christianity does not contradict but rather actually fulfills Old Testament Judaism.

After establishing his apostolic credentials, Paul made his case for justification by faith alone using a revered Old Testament person (Abraham) and assorted Old Testament passages.

Paul anticipated and refuted a possible objection to his use of Abraham to prove the doctrine of justification by faith: that the giving of the law at Sinai occurred after Abraham and brought about a change and a better method of salvation. The apostle dismissed that argument by showing the superiority of the Abrahamic Covenant (verses 15–18) and the inferiority of the law (verses 19–22).

Paul again emphasized that there is no middle ground between law (works) and promise (grace); the two principles are mutually exclusive (see Romans 4:14). An "inheritance" is by definition something granted, not worked for, as proven in the case of Abraham.

Bible Passage

Read 3:10–18, noting the key words and definitions to the right of the passage.

Galatians 3:10–18

10 *For as many as are of the works of the law are under the curse; for it is written, "Cursed is everyone who does not continue in all things which are written in the book of the law, to do them."*

as many as are of the works of the law (v. 10)—those attempting to earn salvation by keeping the law

under the curse (v. 10)—quoted from Deuteronomy 27:26

¹¹ But that no one is justified by the law in the sight of God is evident, for "the just shall live by faith."

¹² Yet the law is not of faith, but "the man who does them shall live by them."

¹³ Christ has redeemed us from the curse of the law, having become a curse for us (for it is written, "Cursed is everyone who hangs on a tree"),

¹⁴ that the blessing of Abraham might come upon the Gentiles in Christ Jesus, that we might receive the promise of the Spirit through faith.

¹⁵ Brethren, I speak in the manner of men: Though it is only a man's covenant, yet if it is confirmed, no one annuls or adds to it.

¹⁶ Now to Abraham and his Seed were the promises made. He does not say, "And to seeds," as of many, but as of one, "And to your Seed," who is Christ.

¹⁷ And this I say, that the law, which was four hundred and thirty years later, cannot annul the covenant that was confirmed before by God in Christ, that it should make the promise of no effect.

¹⁸ For if the inheritance is of the law, it is no longer of promise; but God gave it to Abraham by promise.

to show that failure to perfectly keep the law brings divine judgment and condemnation; one violation of the law deserves the curse of God (see Deuteronomy 27–28)

all things (v. 10)—See James 2:10. No one can keep all the commands of the law—not even strict Pharisees like Saul of Tarsus.

justified (v. 11)—made righteous before God

the just shall live by faith (v. 11)—Paul's earlier Old Testament quote (verse 10; see Deuteronomy 27:26) showed that justification does not come from keeping the law. This quote from Habakkuk 2:4 shows that justification is by faith alone.

the law is not of faith (v. 12) —Justification by faith and justification by keeping the law are mutually exclusive, as Paul's Old Testament quote from Leviticus 18:5 proves.

Christ has redeemed us from the curse of the law (v. 13)— The Greek word translated "redeemed" was often used to speak of buying a slave's or debtor's freedom. Christ's death, because it was a death of substitution for sin, satisfied God's justice and exhausted His wrath toward His elect, so that Christ actually purchased believers from slavery to sin and from the sentence of eternal death (Titus 2:14; see Romans 3:24; Ephesians 1:7).

having become a curse for us (v. 13)—By bearing God's wrath for believers' sins on the cross, Christ took upon Himself the curse pronounced on those who violated the law.

it is written (v. 13)—the common New Testament way (used sixty-one times) of introducing Old Testament quotes

the blessing of Abraham (v. 14)—faith in God's promise of salvation

promise of the Spirit (v. 14)—from God the Father (see Isaiah 32:15; Ezekiel 37:14; Luke 11:13; 24:49; John 14:16, 26)

Brethren (v. 15)—This term of endearment reveals Paul's compassionate love for the Galatians, which they may have begun to question in light of his stern rebuke (verses 1, 3).

manner of men . . . man's covenant (v. 15)—Even human covenants, once confirmed, are considered irrevocable and unchangeable; how much more a covenant made by an unchanging God (James 1:17).

Seed (v. 16)—See verse 19; the quote is from Genesis 12:7. The singular form of the Hebrew word, like its English and Greek counterparts, can be used in a collective sense, that is, to refer to a group. Paul's point is that in some Old Testament passages (for example, Genesis 3:15; 22:18), "seed" refers to the greatest of Abraham's descendants, Jesus Christ.

promises (v. 16)—those associated with the Abrahamic Covenant (Genesis 12:3, 7; 13:15–16; 15:5, 18; 17:8; 22:16–18; 26:3–4; 28:13–14). Because these promises were made both to Abraham and to his descendants, they did not become void when Abraham died or when the law came.

four hundred and thirty years (v. 17)—from Israel's sojourn in Egypt (see Exodus 12:40) to the giving of the law at Sinai (1445 B.C.); the law actually came 645 years after the initial promise to Abraham (2090 B.C.; see Genesis 12:4; 21:5; 25:26; 47:9), but the promise was repeated to Isaac (Genesis 26:24) and later to Jacob (1928 B.C.; Genesis 28:15); the last known reaffirmation of the Abrahamic Covenant to Jacob occurred in Genesis 46:2–4 (1875 B.C.) just before he went to Egypt—430 years before the Mosaic law was given.

the covenant (v. 17)—the Abrahamic Covenant

confirmed before by God (v. 17)—The term means "ratified." Once God ratified the covenant officially, it had lasting authority so that nothing and no one could annul it. The Abrahamic Covenant was unilateral (God made the promise to Himself), eternal (it provided for everlasting blessing), irrevocable (it will never cease), and unconditional (in that it depended on God, not man), but its complete fulfillment awaits the salvation of Israel and the millennial kingdom of Jesus Christ.

Understanding the Text

4) How does Paul contrast the law and faith? What does Paul say is the destiny of the one who fails to keep 100 percent of the law?

_____

_____

_____

_____

_____

_____

5) What does it mean that Christ "redeemed us"?

_____

_____

_____

_____

_____

_____

(verses to consider: 1 Corinthians 1:30; Galatians 4:3–5; Colossians 1:13–14; 1 Peter 1:18–19)

6) How did Christ become "a curse for us"?

_____

_____

_____

_____

_____

_____

(verses to consider: 2 Corinthians 5:21; 1 Peter 2:21–24)

Cross-Reference

Read Romans 7:1–25:

1 *Or do you not know, brethren (for I speak to those who know the law), that the law has dominion over a man as long as he lives?*

2 *For the woman who has a husband is bound by the law to her husband as long as he lives. But if the husband dies, she is released from the law of her husband.*

3 *So then if, while her husband lives, she marries another man, she will be called an adulteress; but if her husband dies, she is free from that law, so that she is no adulteress, though she has married another man.*

⁴ *Therefore, my brethren, you also have become dead to the law through the body of Christ, that you may be married to another—to Him who was raised from the dead, that we should bear fruit to God.*

⁵ *For when we were in the flesh, the sinful passions which were aroused by the law were at work in our members to bear fruit to death.*

⁶ *But now we have been delivered from the law, having died to what we were held by, so that we should serve in the newness of the Spirit and not in the oldness of the letter.*

⁷ *What shall we say then? Is the law sin? Certainly not! On the contrary, I would not have known sin except through the law. For I would not have known covetousness unless the law had said, "You shall not covet."*

⁸ *But sin, taking opportunity by the commandment, produced in me all manner of evil desire. For apart from the law sin was dead.*

⁹ *I was alive once without the law, but when the commandment came, sin revived and I died.*

¹⁰ *And the commandment, which was to bring life, I found to bring death.*

¹¹ *For sin, taking occasion by the commandment, deceived me, and by it killed me.*

¹² *Therefore the law is holy, and the commandment holy and just and good.*

¹³ *Has then what is good become death to me? Certainly not! But sin, that it might appear sin, was producing death in me through what is good, so that sin through the commandment might become exceedingly sinful.*

¹⁴ *For we know that the law is spiritual, but I am carnal, sold under sin.*

¹⁵ *For what I am doing, I do not understand. For what I will to do, that I do not practice; but what I hate, that I do.*

¹⁶ *If, then, I do what I will not to do, I agree with the law that it is good.*

¹⁷ *But now, it is no longer I who do it, but sin that dwells in me.*

¹⁸ *For I know that in me (that is, in my flesh) nothing good dwells; for to will is present with me, but how to perform what is good I do not find.*

¹⁹ *For the good that I will to do, I do not do; but the evil I will not to do, that I practice.*

²⁰ *Now if I do what I will not to do, it is no longer I who do it, but sin that dwells in me.*

²¹ *I find then a law, that evil is present with me, the one who wills to do good.*

²² *For I delight in the law of God according to the inward man.*

²³ *But I see another law in my members, warring against the law of my mind, and bringing me into captivity to the law of sin which is in my members.*

²⁴ *O wretched man that I am! Who will deliver me from this body of death?*

²⁵ *I thank God—through Jesus Christ our Lord! So then, with the mind I myself serve the law of God, but with the flesh the law of sin.*

7) In what ways do Paul's words in Romans 7 echo the principles being taught in 3:10–18?

_____

_____

_____

_____

_____

_____

Exploring the Meaning

8) Read John 7:37–39. Instead of a cold, external law, what did Christ promise those who would trust and obey Him?

_____

_____

_____

_____

_____

(verses to consider: Isaiah 44:3; Ezekiel 36:26–27; 39:29; Joel 2:28–29)

9) Read Hebrews 10:38. How does this verse demonstrate that justification is by faith alone?

_____

_____

_____

_____

_____

Summing Up...

"Whether before or after Christ came to our earth, salvation has always been provided only through the perfect offering of Christ on the cross. Believers who lived before the cross and never knew any specifics about Jesus were nevertheless forgiven and made right with God by faith in anticipation of Christ's sacrifice, whereas believers who live after the cross are saved in looking back to it. When Christ shed His blood, it covered sins on both sides of the cross. The Old Covenant goes back to the cross; the New Covenant comes from it. On the one hand faith pointed forward, whereas on the other it points back."—*John MacArthur*

Reflecting on the Text

10) When have you felt spiritually overwhelmed or frustrated because of your inability to live up to God's standard? How did you resolve this? What would Paul say to those who are religiously frustrated?

_____

_____

_____

_____

_____

_____

11) What different kinds of words describe these two different scenes: a rebellious child being punished by a parent; a reconciled child being given a priceless inheritance? How does this lesson, in a sense, paint this contrasting picture?

_____

_____

_____

_____

_____

_____

_____

12) List the names of those in your life who desperately need to know that salvation is a gift and can't be earned. Commit to pray for them. Ask God for opportunities to share Christ's message of love and grace with them.

_____

_____

_____

_____

_____

_____

Recording Your Thoughts

_____

_____

_____

_____

_____

_____

_____

_____

_____

_____

For further study, see the following verses:

Genesis 15:18–21	Leviticus 18:5	Deuteronomy 21:23; 27:26
Isaiah 59:19–21	Habakkuk 2:4	Malachi 3:6
Romans 1:17; 3:20–24;	Romans 7:7–12; 9:4	Hebrews 9:12
James 2:10	1 Peter 3:18	

The Purpose of the Law

Opening Thought

1) If, as many argue, people are inherently good, why do we need policemen, jails, prisons, criminal courts, handcuffs, etc.?

_____

_____

_____

_____

2) What laws, regulations, or ordinances do many people (even many Christians) routinely break? Why?

_____

_____

_____

_____

3) What does it mean if every time you see a police officer while driving, you instinctively take your foot off the accelerator, look down at your dashboard, and lightly touch the brake pedal?

_____

_____

_____

_____

Background of the Passage

Paul wrote this urgent letter to churches he had established in Asia Minor on his first missionary journey. Shortly after he had left them, these churches were targeted by Jewish legalists who, in essence, urged the believers in Christ to turn away from grace and embrace the tenets of Judaism, especially the rite of circumcision and a fanatical devotion to keeping the law of Moses. These "Judaizers" were trying to discredit Paul and, in the process, cast doubts on the gospel he preached.

Paul saw these developments as nothing less than an assault on the simplicity and purity of the gospel of grace. Because the eternal and theological implications of such teaching were grave, the brilliant apostle responded with stern words of rebuke and clear teaching on the distinctions between law and grace.

Paul knew his readers would reason: "Well, if the law can't save us, why did God give the law in the first place? What's its purpose? And if the law has been set aside, are we free of any and all moral restraints?" The result is 3:19–29—a clear and concise explanation of the purpose of the law. Without the law, people are incapable of seeing their depravity and need for forgiveness. When the law is obscured, grace appears less amazing than it actually is.

This section (3:19–29) ends on a wonderfully encouraging note. It speaks of the freedom that believers enjoy, the sonship they have, the unity they have been granted, and the inheritance that is theirs—not because they are able to keep God's laws but because of the grace of God that comes through faith in Christ.

Bible Passage

Read 3:19–29, noting the key words and definitions to the right of the passage.

Galatians 3:19–29

¹⁹ *What purpose then does the law serve? It was added because of transgressions, till the Seed should come to whom the promise was made; and it was appointed through angels by the hand of a mediator.*

was added because of transgressions (v. 19)—Paul's persuasive argument that the promise is superior to the law raises an obvious question: What was the purpose of the law? Paul's answer is that the law reveals humanity's utter sinfulness, inability to save themselves, and desperate need

20 *Now a mediator does not mediate for one only, but God is one.*

21 *Is the law then against the promises of God? Certainly not! For if there had been a law given which could have given life, truly righteousness would have been by the law.*

22 *But the Scripture has confined all under sin, that the promise by faith in Jesus Christ might be given to those who believe.*

23 *But before faith came, we were kept under guard by the law, kept for the faith which would afterward be revealed.*

24 *Therefore the law was our tutor to bring us to Christ, that we might be justified by faith.*

25 *But after faith has come, we are no longer under a tutor.*

26 *For you are all sons of God through faith in Christ Jesus.*

27 *For as many of you as were baptized into Christ have put on Christ.*

28 *There is neither Jew nor Greek, there is neither slave nor free, there is neither male nor female; for you are all one in Christ Jesus.*

29 *And if you are Christ's, then you are Abraham's seed, and heirs according to the promise.*

of a Savior—it was never intended to be the way of salvation.

through angels (v. 19)—The Bible teaches that angels were involved in the giving of the law (see Hebrews 2:2) but does not explain the precise role they played.

mediator (v. 20)—Paul's point is apparently that a "mediator" is required when more than one party is involved, but God alone ratified the covenant with Abraham.

Certainly not! (v. 21)—Paul uses the strongest Greek negative (see 2:17) to disdain the idea that the law and the promise are at opposite purposes. Since God gave them both and does not work against Himself, law and promise work in harmony; the law reveals humans' sinfulness and need for the salvation freely offered in the promise. If the law could have provided righteousness and eternal life, there would be no gracious promise.

confined all under sin (v. 22) —The Greek verb translated "confined" means "to enclose on all sides." Paul portrays all humankind as hopelessly trapped in sin, like a school of fish caught in a net; that all people are sinners is the express teaching of Scripture (Isaiah 53:6; Romans 3:23).

before faith came (v. 23)— From the viewpoints of both the history of redemption and through all times in the area of individual salvation (verses 19, 24–25; 4:1–4), only saving faith unlocks the door of the prison where the law keeps men and women bound.

kept under guard by the law (v. 23)—Paul personifies the law as a jailer of guilty, condemned sinners, on death row awaiting God's judgment.

the faith which would afterward be revealed (v. 23)—Again, Paul was looking at the coming of Christ, historically, and at each believer's salvation, individually. Faith in Christ alone releases people from bondage to law, whether the Mosaic law or the law written on the hearts of Gentiles.

tutor (v. 24)—The Greek word denotes a slave who had the duty of taking care of a child until adulthood. The "tutor" would escort the children to and from school and watch over their behavior at home. Tutors were often strict disciplinarians, causing those under their care to yearn for the day when they would be free from their tutor's custody. The law, our tutor, by showing us our sins, was escorting us to Christ.

sons of God (v. 26)—While God is the Father of all people in a general sense because He created them (Acts 17:24–28), only those who have put their faith in Jesus Christ are God's true spiritual children; unbelievers are the children of Satan (1 John 3:10).

baptized into Christ (v. 27)—This is not water baptism, which cannot save. Paul used the word "baptized" in a metaphorical manner to speak of being "placed into" Christ (see 2:20) by the spiritual miracle of union with Him in His death and resurrection.

put on Christ (v. 27)—the result of the believer's spiritual union with Christ; Paul was emphasizing the fact that we have been united with Christ through salvation; positionally before God, we have put on Christ, His death, resurrection, and righteousness; practically, we need to "put on Christ" before people, in our conduct (Romans 13:14).

you are all one in Christ Jesus (v. 28)—All those who are one with Jesus Christ are one with each other. This verse does not deny that God has designed racial, social, and sexual distinctions among Christians, but it affirms that those distinctions do not imply spiritual inequality before God; nor is this spiritual equality incompatible with the God-ordained roles of headship and submission in the church, society, and at home. Jesus Christ, though fully equal with the Father, assumed a submissive role during His incarnation (Philippians 2:5–8).

Understanding the Text

4) Underline every word or phrase that refers to or describes the law. How does Paul describe the law in this passage? What does he suggest is its purpose?

_____

_____

_____

_____

_____

5) What does this passage say about the universality of sin or the depravity of the human race? Is anyone able to keep the perfect law of God?

_____

_____

_____

_____

_____

(verses to consider: 1 Kings 8:46; Psalm 143:2; Romans 3:9–23)

6) What does this passage say about who are the "sons of God"?

_____

_____

_____

_____

(verses to consider: Romans 8:14–17)

7) What does it mean to be "baptized into Christ" (verse 27)?

_____

_____

_____

_____

_____

(verses to consider: Romans 6:3–5)

Cross-Reference

Read Matthew 5:17–48:

[17] *"Do not think that I came to destroy the Law or the Prophets. I did not come to destroy but to fulfill.*

¹⁸ *For assuredly, I say to you, till heaven and earth pass away, one jot or one tittle will by no means pass from the law till all is fulfilled.*

¹⁹ *Whoever therefore breaks one of the least of these commandments, and teaches men so, shall be called least in the kingdom of heaven; but whoever does and teaches them, he shall be called great in the kingdom of heaven.*

²⁰ *For I say to you, that unless your righteousness exceeds the righteousness of the scribes and Pharisees, you will by no means enter the kingdom of heaven.*

²¹ *You have heard that it was said to those of old, 'You shall not murder, and whoever murders will be in danger of the judgment.'*

²² *But I say to you that whoever is angry with his brother without a cause shall be in danger of the judgment. And whoever says to his brother, 'Raca!' shall be in danger of the council. But whoever says, 'You fool!' shall be in danger of hell fire.*

²³ *Therefore if you bring your gift to the altar, and there remember that your brother has something against you,*

²⁴ *leave your gift there before the altar, and go your way. First be reconciled to your brother, and then come and offer your gift.*

²⁵ *Agree with your adversary quickly, while you are on the way with him, lest your adversary deliver you to the judge, the judge hand you over to the officer, and you be thrown into prison.*

²⁶ *Assuredly, I say to you, you will by no means get out of there till you have paid the last penny.*

²⁷ *You have heard that it was said to those of old, 'You shall not commit adultery.'*

²⁸ *But I say to you that whoever looks at a woman to lust for her has already committed adultery with her in his heart.*

²⁹ *If your right eye causes you to sin, pluck it out and cast it from you; for it is more profitable for you that one of your members perish, than for your whole body to be cast into hell.*

³⁰ *And if your right hand causes you to sin, cut it off and cast it from you; for it is more profitable for you that one of your members perish, than for your whole body to be cast into hell.*

³¹ *Furthermore it has been said, 'Whoever divorces his wife, let him give her a certificate of divorce.'*

³² *But I say to you that whoever divorces his wife for any reason except sexual immorality causes her to commit adultery; and whoever marries a woman who is divorced commits adultery.*

³³ *Again you have heard that it was said to those of old, 'You shall not swear falsely, but shall perform your oaths to the Lord.'*

³⁴ *But I say to you, do not swear at all: neither by heaven, for it is God's throne;*

³⁵ *nor by the earth, for it is His footstool; nor by Jerusalem, for it is the city of the great King.*

³⁶ *Nor shall you swear by your head, because you cannot make one hair white or black.*

³⁷ *But let your 'Yes' be 'Yes,' and your 'No,' 'No.' For whatever is more than these is from the evil one.*

³⁸ *You have heard that it was said, 'An eye for an eye and a tooth for a tooth.'*

³⁹ *But I tell you not to resist an evil person. But whoever slaps you on your right cheek, turn the other to him also.*

⁴⁰ *If anyone wants to sue you and take away your tunic, let him have your cloak also.*

⁴¹ *And whoever compels you to go one mile, go with him two.*

⁴² *Give to him who asks you, and from him who wants to borrow from you do not turn away.*

⁴³ *You have heard that it was said, 'You shall love your neighbor and hate your enemy.'*

⁴⁴ *But I say to you, love your enemies, bless those who curse you, do good to those who hate you, and pray for those who spitefully use you and persecute you,*

⁴⁵ *that you may be sons of your Father in heaven; for He makes His sun rise on the evil and on the good, and sends rain on the just and on the unjust.*

⁴⁶ *For if you love those who love you, what reward have you? Do not even the tax collectors do the same?*

⁴⁷ *And if you greet your brethren only, what do you do more than others? Do not even the tax collectors do so?*

⁴⁸ *Therefore you shall be perfect, just as your Father in heaven is perfect."*

8) How did the Jewish religious leaders feel when they heard Jesus require not only perfect external but absolute internal conformity to the law of God?

_____

_____

_____

_____

_____

_____

Exploring the Meaning

9) Read Romans 6:23. How does the image there fit with the description in Galatians 3 of being "kept under guard by the law," of the law serving as a kind of death-row prison?

_____

_____

_____

_____

_____

_____

_____

_____

10) Read Romans 2:12–16. How does the law written on the hearts of Gentiles compare with the law revealed by God through Moses?

_____

_____

_____

_____

_____

Summing Up...

"The covenant of law is long past, but the moral demands of the law have not diminished, having neither begun nor ended with the Mosaic covenant. That is why preaching the moral, ethical standards of the law today is still imperative in driving men to Christ. Unless men realize they are living in violation of God's law and therefore stand under His divine judgment, they will see no reason to be saved. Grace is meaningless to a person who feels no inadequacy or need of help. He sees no purpose in being saved if he does not realize he is lost. He sees no need of forgiveness by God if he does not know he has offended God. He sees no need to seek God's mercy if he is unaware he is under God's wrath.

"The purpose of the law was, and is, to drive men to despair over their sins and to a desire to receive the salvation that God's sovereign grace offers to those who believe."—_John MacArthur_

Reflecting on the Text

11) John Stott has written: "We cannot come to Christ to be justified until we have first been to Moses to be condemned. But once we have gone to Moses, and acknowledged our sin, guilt, and condemnation, we must not stay there. We must let Moses send us to Christ" (*The Message of Galatians* [London: InterVarsity, 1968], p. 102; cited in MacArthur, *Galatians*, p. 101).

Instead of the futility of trying to keep the impossible demands of the law, Paul urges believers to "put on Christ" (verse 27; also see Romans 13:14). What would this look like in your life today? How does one do this?

_____

_____

_____

_____

_____

_____

_____

12) What are the blessings of being a "son of God"? How can you live in such a way today that your Father is honored and glorified?

_____

_____

_____

_____

_____

_____

_____

13) What central truth stands out in your mind from this lesson? Summarize that idea in your own words:

_____

_____

_____

_____

_____

_____

Recording Your Thoughts

_____

_____

_____

_____

_____

_____

_____

_____

_____

_____

_____

_____

_____

For further study, see the following verses:

Genesis 15:7–21	Ecclesiastes 7:20	Acts 2:38; 7:53; 22:16
Romans 7:1–13	Ephesians 2:3	Philippians 3:8–10
1 John 5:19		

Sons of God

Opening Thought

1) Imagine that you're visiting with a neighbor and somehow the conversation turns to spiritual things. At one point your neighbor exclaims, "Well, I believe we're all children of God. He created us all and loves us all, whether we're Christian, Jewish, Hindu, or Muslim." How would you respond tactfully?

_____

_____

_____

_____

_____

2) Imagine living in another time and being a slave. What do you think your life would be like? Imagine living at that same time, but instead of being a slave, being a child of the king. What would your life be like in that circumstance? Why?

_____

_____

_____

_____

_____

_____

Background of the Passage

Paul wrote this epistle to combat the influence of a group known as the Judaizers who had infiltrated the churches of Asia Minor. These false teachers were confusing believers by insisting that, in addition to belief in Christ, it was necessary for them to adhere to all Jewish rites and practices if they wished to be saved.

Continuing his basic argument that salvation is not gained by human merit or works but solely by God's sovereign grace through faith, Paul further developed the analogy of a child becoming an adult (3:23–26). He compared the position and privileges of a child to those of a servant, with the figures of child and servant representing life under the law and the figures of adult and son representing life in Christ. Both Paul's Jewish and Gentile readers readily understood this imagery, since the Jews, Greeks, and Romans all had a ceremony to celebrate a person's coming of age.

The central truths of 4:1–11 are that life under law is meant by God to be preparation for divine sonship and that trust in His grace brings realization of that sonship.

While salvation is the free gift of God (Romans 5:15–16, 18), it brings with it serious responsibility. God requires believers to live holy lives because they are children of a holy God and should want to love and worship Him. This obligation to the unchanging moral and spiritual principles that forever reflect the nature of God, however, does not include the rituals and ceremonies unique to Israel under Mosaic law, as the Judaizers falsely claimed.

Bible Passage

Read 4:1–11, noting the key words and definitions to the right of the passage.

Galatians 4:1–11

¹ *Now I say that the heir, as long as he is a child, does not differ at all from a slave, though he is master of all,*

² *but is under guardians and stewards until the time appointed by the father.*

child (v. 1)—The Greek word refers to a child too young to talk; a minor, spiritually and intellectually immature and not ready for the privileges and responsibilities of adulthood.

guardians and stewards (v. 2)—"Guardians" were slaves

³ Even so we, when we were children, were in bondage under the elements of the world.

⁴ But when the fullness of the time had come, God sent forth His Son, born of a woman, born under the law,

⁵ to redeem those who were under the law, that we might receive the adoption as sons.

⁶ And because you are sons, God has sent forth the Spirit of His Son into your hearts, crying out, "Abba, Father!"

⁷ Therefore you are no longer a slave but a son, and if a son, then an heir of God through Christ.

⁸ But then, indeed, when you did not know God, you served those which by nature are not gods.

⁹ But now after you have known God, or rather are known by God, how is it that you turn again to the weak and beggarly elements, to which you desire again to be in bondage?

¹⁰ You observe days and months and seasons and years.

¹¹ I am afraid for you, lest I have labored for you in vain.

entrusted with the care of under-age boys, while "stewards" managed property for the boys until they came of age. Along with the tutor (3:24), they had almost complete charge of the child—so that, for all practical purposes, a child under their care did not differ from a slave.

when we were children . . . in bondage (v. 3)—before our "coming of age" when we came to saving faith in Jesus Christ

the elements of the world (v. 3)—"Elements" is from a Greek word meaning "row," or "rank," and was used to speak of basic, foundational things like the letters of the alphabet. In light of its use in verse 9, it is best to see it here as a reference to the basic elements and rituals of human religion. Paul describes both Jewish and Gentile religions as elemental because they are merely human, never rising to the level of the divine. Both Jewish religion and Gentile religion centered on human-made systems of works; they were filled with laws and ceremonies to be performed so as to achieve divine acceptance. All such rudimentary elements are immature, like behaviors of children under bondage to a guardian.

the fullness of the time (v. 4) —In God's timetable, when the exact religious, cultural, and political conditions demanded by His perfect plan were in place, Jesus came into the world.

God sent forth His Son (v. 4) —Just as a father would set the time for the ceremony of his son coming of age and being released from the guardians, stewards, and tutors, so God sent His Son at the precise moment to bring all who believe out from under bondage to the law—a truth Jesus repeatedly affirmed (John 5:30, 36–37; 8:16, 18, 42; 12:49; 17:21, 25; 20:21).

That the Father sent Jesus into the world implies Jesus' preexistence as the eternal second member of the Trinity.

born of a woman (v. 4)—This emphasizes Jesus' full humanity, not merely His virgin birth (Isaiah 7:14; Matthew 1:20–25). Jesus had to be fully God for His sacrifice to be of the infinite worth needed to atone for sin, but He also had to be fully man so He could take upon Himself the penalty of sin as the substitute for human beings.

under the law (v. 4)—Like all human beings, Jesus was obligated to obey God's law. Unlike anyone else, however, He perfectly obeyed that law (1 John 3:5). His sinlessness made Him the unblemished sacrifice for sins, who "fulfilled all righteousness" (that is, perfectly obeyed God in everything). That perfect righteousness is what is imputed to those who believe in Him.

those . . . under the law (v. 5)—guilty sinners who are under the law's demands and its curses and in need of a savior

the adoption as sons (v. 5)—"Adoption" is the act of bringing someone who is the offspring of another into one's own family. Since unregenerate people are by nature children of the devil, the only way they can become God's children is by spiritual adoption.

Spirit of His Son (v. 6)—It is the Holy Spirit's work to confirm to believers their adoption as God's children. Assurance of salvation is a gracious work of the Holy Spirit and does not come from any human source.

Abba (v. 6)—an Aramaic term of endearment, used by young children to speak to their fathers; the equivalent of the word "Daddy"

when you did not know God (v. 8)—Before coming to saving faith in Christ, no unsaved person knows God.

by nature are not gods (v. 8)—the Greco-Roman pantheon of nonexistent deities the Galatians had imagined they worshiped before their conversion (see Romans 1:23; 1 Corinthians 8:4; 10:19–20; 12:2; 1 Thessalonians 1:9)

known by God (v. 9)—We can know God only because He first knew us, just as we choose Him only because He first chose us (John 6:44; 15:16), and we love Him only because He first loved us (1 John 4:19).

days . . . years (v. 10)—the rituals, ceremonies, and festivals of the Jewish religious calendar that God had given to Israel but were never required for the church; Paul warns the Galatians, as he did the Colossians, against legalistically observing them as if they were required by God or could earn favor with Him.

labored . . . in vain (v. 11)—Paul feared that his effort in establishing and building the Galatian churches might prove to be futile if they fell back into legalism.

Understanding the Text

3) How does Paul say that being under the law prepared us for sonship? To what ancient practice is he referring when he implies that the law functioned as a guardian or manager?

_____

_____

_____

_____

_____

_____

4) Like all humanity, Jesus was born under the law (verse 4). But how was Christ different from other people in his relationship and response to the law?

_____

_____

_____

_____

_____

(verses to consider: John 8:46; 2 Corinthians 5:21; Hebrews 4:15; 7:26; 1 Peter 2:22)

5) What does it mean that God adopted us? How does God's Spirit confirm this fact?

_____

_____

_____

_____

_____

(verses to consider: Romans 8:15–17; Ephesians 1:4–5)

6) What concern did Paul express over the Galatians and their legalistic behavior?

_____

_____

_____

_____

_____

_____

Cross-Reference

Read Romans 8:1–17

1 *There is therefore now no condemnation to those who are in Christ Jesus, who do not walk according to the flesh, but according to the Spirit.*

2 *For the law of the Spirit of life in Christ Jesus has made me free from the law of sin and death.*

3 *For what the law could not do in that it was weak through the flesh, God did by sending His own Son in the likeness of sinful flesh, on account of sin: He condemned sin in the flesh,*

4 *that the righteous requirement of the law might be fulfilled in us who do not walk according to the flesh but according to the Spirit.*

5 *For those who live according to the flesh set their minds on the things of the flesh, but those who live according to the Spirit, the things of the Spirit.*

6 *For to be carnally minded is death, but to be spiritually minded is life and peace.*

7 *Because the carnal mind is enmity against God; for it is not subject to the law of God, nor indeed can be.*

8 *So then, those who are in the flesh cannot please God.*

9 *But you are not in the flesh but in the Spirit, if indeed the Spirit of God dwells in you. Now if anyone does not have the Spirit of Christ, he is not His.*

10 *And if Christ is in you, the body is dead because of sin, but the Spirit is life because of righteousness.*

11 *But if the Spirit of Him who raised Jesus from the dead dwells in you, He who raised Christ from the dead will also give life to your mortal bodies through His Spirit who dwells in you.*

¹² *Therefore, brethren, we are debtors—not to the flesh, to live according to the flesh.*

¹³ *For if you live according to the flesh you will die; but if by the Spirit you put to death the deeds of the body, you will live.*

¹⁴ *For as many as are led by the Spirit of God, these are sons of God.*

¹⁵ *For you did not receive the spirit of bondage again to fear, but you received the Spirit of adoption by whom we cry out, "Abba, Father."*

¹⁶ *The Spirit Himself bears witness with our spirit that we are children of God,*

¹⁷ *and if children, then heirs—heirs of God and joint heirs with Christ, if indeed we suffer with Him, that we may also be glorified together.*

7) What extra insights into sonship does Romans 8 add to the teaching of Galatians 3?

_____

_____

_____

_____

_____

_____

Exploring the Meaning

8) Read Ephesians 4:17–19. Is it possible to know God apart from believing in Christ? How do you know?

_____

_____

_____

_____

_____

(verses to consider: John 8:28–47; 2 Corinthians 4:3–6; Ephesians 2:1–10; 1 John 4:19)

9) Read Romans 14:1–8, 14–18. Are any Jewish rituals, customs, or holy days required for the church and modern-day believers? How do you know?

_____

_____

_____

_____

_____

_____

(verses to consider: Colossians 2:16–17)

Summing Up...

Because believers are God's children, they are then heirs, "heirs of God and joint heirs with Christ" (Romans 8:17). What an incomprehensible truth: that by giving ourselves to Jesus Christ in faith, God gives us everything His Son possesses!

"The gracious gift of sonship is free, but it brings serious obligation. Great blessing carries great responsibility (Luke 12:48)."—_John MacArthur_

Reflecting on the Text

10) How do you know that you are a child of God? How can you be sure? How can any believer have assurance?

_____

_____

_____

_____

11) How faithfully are you living as an adopted heir of the King of the universe? What practical differences should this biblical truth make in your life today?

_____

_____

_____

_____

_____

_____

12) What "weak and worthless elemental things" are you tempted to do in order to please God or somehow "earn" His approval? What do you think has caused you to view these behaviors or practices as necessary to a life that honors God?

_____

_____

_____

_____

_____

_____

_____

Recording Your Thoughts

_____

_____

_____

_____

_____

_____

_____

_____

_____

_____

_____

_____

_____

For further study, see the following verses:

Matthew 5:48	Luke 1:32, 35; 12:48	John 1:1, 14, 18; 6:39, 44, 57
Romans 6:23; 8:3–4	Ephesians 2:8	Philippians 2:6–7
Colossians 2:8	1 Thessalonians 3:5	Hebrews 1:3–5
1 Peter 1:15–18		

Christ in You

Opening Thought

1) Whom do people say that you remind them of? Anyone famous? Is it mostly your appearance or your mannerisms?

_____

_____

_____

_____

_____

_____

2) When did your heart absolutely ache for someone due to a pattern of stubborn, foolish, or naïve choices you observed in their lives (and the potentially devastating consequences of those decisions)?

_____

_____

_____

_____

_____

_____

_____

Background of the Passage

Until this point, Paul's approach has been confrontational and impersonal. He has been writing like a scholar or debater, marshaling every possible argument and illustration to get his message across. He has taken the stance of a determined lawyer in court or a learned theologian in the classroom, giving a dispassionate and irrefutable presentation. He has referred to the Old Testament to teach the Galatians the basic truth of the gospel that he had taught them many times before: Salvation is by God's grace through faith alone. He has used both his own experience and that of the Galatians to reinforce his teaching. But for the most part, he has sounded detached, seeming to be more concerned about principles than people.

The apostle's approach changed dramatically in 4:12. His anger at the Judaizers subsided, and he moved from the purely doctrinal to the more personal. In fact, verses 12–20 are Paul's strongest words of personal affection in any of his letters. He did not so much preach or teach as simply pour out his heart in personal exhortation. He wrote, in effect, "I care about you more than I can say. I love you dearly just as you have loved me dearly. Please listen to what I'm saying, because it's so vitally essential."

In the course of his intimate outpouring to the Galatians in 4:12–20, Paul first appealed to them, then fondly remembered their loving acceptance of him; he warned them about the ulterior motives of the Judaizers and finally told them of his desire to be with them again in person.

Bible Passage

Read 4:12–20, noting the key words and definitions to the right of the passage.

Galatians 4:12–20

12 *Brethren, I urge you to become like me, for I became like you. You have not injured me at all.*

13 *You know that because of physical infirmity I preached the gospel to you at the first.*

14 *And my trial which was in my flesh you did not despise or reject, but you received me as an angel of God, even as Christ Jesus.*

become like me, for I became like you (v. 12)—Paul had been a proud, self-righteous Pharisee, trusting in his own righteousness to save him (see Philippians 3:4–6). But when he came to Christ, he abandoned all efforts to save himself, trusting wholly in God's grace (Philippians 3:7–9). He urged the Galatians to follow his example and avoid the legalism of the Judaizers.

15 *What then was the blessing you enjoyed? For I bear you witness that, if possible, you would have plucked out your own eyes and given them to me.*

16 *Have I therefore become your enemy because I tell you the truth?*

17 *They zealously court you, but for no good; yes, they want to exclude you, that you may be zealous for them.*

18 *But it is good to be zealous in a good thing always, and not only when I am present with you.*

19 *My little children, for whom I labor in birth again until Christ is formed in you,*

20 *I would like to be present with you now and to change my tone; for I have doubts about you.*

You have not injured me (v. 12)—Though the Jews had persecuted him during his first trip to Galatia, the Galatian believers had not harmed Paul but had enthusiastically received him when he preached the gospel to them (see Acts 14:19). So he asked how they could reject him now.

physical infirmity (v. 13)—Some think the illness to which Paul was referring was malaria, possibly contracted in the coastal lowlands of Pamphylia. That could explain why Paul and Barnabas apparently did not preach at Perga, a city in Pamphylia (see Acts 13:13–14). The cooler and healthier weather in Galatia and especially at Pisidian Antioch (3,600 feet above sea level), where Paul went when he left Perga, would have brought some relief to the fever caused by malaria. Although malaria is a serious, debilitating disease, its attacks are not continuous; Paul could have ministered between bouts.

you received me (v. 14)—The Galatians had welcomed Paul in spite of his illness, which in no way had been a barrier to his credibility or acceptance.

blessing you enjoyed (v. 15)—"Blessing" can also be translated "happiness" or "satisfaction." Paul points out that the Galatians had been happy and content with his gospel preaching (see Acts 13:48), so he wondered why they had turned against him.

plucked out your own eyes (v. 15)—This may be a figure of speech (see Matthew 18:9) or an indication that Paul's bodily illness had somehow affected his eyes (see Gal. 6:11). In either case, it reflects the great love the Galatians had initially expressed for the apostle.

your enemy (v. 16)—The Galatians had become so confused that, despite their previous affection for Paul, some had come to regard him as their enemy. The apostle reminds them that he had not harmed them but merely had told them the truth—a truth that had once brought them great joy.

They (v. 17)—the Judaizers

zealously (v. 17)—with a serious concern, or warm interest (the same word is used in 1:14 to describe Paul's former zeal for Judaism); the Judaizers appeared to have a genuine interest in the Galatians, but their true motive was to exclude the Galatians from God's gracious salvation and win recognition for themselves.

not only when I am present (v. 18)—Paul encouraged the Galatians to have the same zeal for the true gospel of grace that they had had when he was with them.

My little children (v. 19)—Paul's only use of this affectionate phrase, which John uses frequently (1 John 2:1, 18, 28; 3:7; 4:4; 5:21)

until Christ is formed in you (v. 19)—In contrast to the evil motives of the Judaizers, Paul sought to bring the Galatians to Christlikeness—the goal of salvation.

doubts (v. 20)—The verb means "to be at wits end" (see verse 6).

Understanding the Text

3) When Paul urged the Galatians to "become as I am," did he mean they were to: (a) become missionaries; (b) become free from the pressure to conform to the law; (c) become circumcised? How do you know?

_____

_____

_____

_____

_____

_____

(verses to consider: 1 Corinthians 9:20–22; Gal. 2:19; 5:1; Ephesians 2:6–10)

4) What memories of his time in Galatia did Paul relate? What is significant about these actions on the part of the Galatian church?

_____

_____

_____

_____

_____

_____

_____

(verses to consider: Acts 13:43—14:1)

5) Many have speculated about the nature of Paul's illness (that he only mentions here in passing). Why do many scholars believe that Paul may have suffered from some type of eye ailment?

_____

_____

_____

_____

_____

_____

(verses to consider: 2 Corinthians 12:7–9; Galatians 6:11; Romans 16:22)

Cross-Reference

Read Matthew 23:1–28:

1 *Then Jesus spoke to the multitudes and to His disciples,*
2 *saying: "The scribes and the Pharisees sit in Moses' seat.*
3 *Therefore whatever they tell you to observe, that observe and do, but do not do according to their works; for they say, and do not do.*
4 *For they bind heavy burdens, hard to bear, and lay them on men's shoulders; but they themselves will not move them with one of their fingers.*

⁵ *But all their works they do to be seen by men. They make their phylacteries broad and enlarge the borders of their garments.*

⁶ *They love the best places at feasts, the best seats in the synagogues,*

⁷ *greetings in the marketplaces, and to be called by men, 'Rabbi, Rabbi.'*

⁸ *But you, do not be called 'Rabbi'; for One is your Teacher, the Christ, and you are all brethren.*

⁹ *Do not call anyone on earth your father; for One is your Father, He who is in heaven.*

¹⁰ *And do not be called teachers; for One is your Teacher, the Christ.*

¹¹ *But he who is greatest among you shall be your servant.*

¹² *And whoever exalts himself will be humbled, and he who humbles himself will be exalted.*

¹³ *But woe to you, scribes and Pharisees, hypocrites! For you shut up the kingdom of heaven against men; for you neither go in yourselves, nor do you allow those who are entering to go in.*

¹⁴ *Woe to you, scribes and Pharisees, hypocrites! For you devour widows' houses, and for a pretense make long prayers. Therefore you will receive greater condemnation.*

¹⁵ *Woe to you, scribes and Pharisees, hypocrites! For you travel land and sea to win one proselyte, and when he is won, you make him twice as much a son of hell as yourselves.*

¹⁶ *Woe to you, blind guides, who say, 'Whoever swears by the temple, it is nothing; but whoever swears by the gold of the temple, he is obliged to perform it.'*

¹⁷ *Fools and blind! For which is greater, the gold or the temple that sanctifies the gold?*

¹⁸ *And, 'Whoever swears by the altar, it is nothing; but whoever swears by the gift that is on it, he is obliged to perform it.'*

¹⁹ *Fools and blind! For which is greater, the gift or the altar that sanctifies the gift?*

²⁰ *Therefore he who swears by the altar, swears by it and by all things on it.*

²¹ *He who swears by the temple, swears by it and by Him who dwells in it.*

²² *And he who swears by heaven, swears by the throne of God and by Him who sits on it.*

²³ *Woe to you, scribes and Pharisees, hypocrites! For you pay tithe of mint and anise and cummin, and have neglected the weightier matters of the law: justice and mercy and faith. These you ought to have done, without leaving the others undone.*

²⁴ *Blind guides, who strain out a gnat and swallow a camel!*

²⁵ *Woe to you, scribes and Pharisees, hypocrites! For you cleanse the outside of the cup and dish, but inside they are full of extortion and self-indulgence.*

²⁶ *Blind Pharisee, first cleanse the inside of the cup and dish, that the outside of them may be clean also.*

27 *Woe to you, scribes and Pharisees, hypocrites! For you are like whitewashed tombs which indeed appear beautiful outwardly, but inside are full of dead men's bones and all uncleanness.*

28 *Even so you also outwardly appear righteous to men, but inside you are full of hypocrisy and lawlessness."*

6) How are the scribes and Pharisees of Matthew 23 similar to the Judaizers as described by Paul in Galatians?

_____

_____

_____

_____

_____

_____

Exploring the Meaning

7) Read 1 Thessalonians 2:7–8. How do Paul's tender words here echo Paul's heart as revealed in 4:19–20? How do these passages square with the common misperception of Paul as being an insensitive and impatient minister of the gospel?

_____

_____

_____

_____

_____

_____

_____

8) Read Romans 8:29. In light of this verse and Galatians 4:19, what is God's goal for believers? What does that mean?

_____

_____

_____

_____

_____

_____

(verses to consider: Romans 13:14; 2 Corinthians 3:18; Colossians 1:28; 2:6; 1 John 3:2)

Summing Up...

"Nothing tears the heart of a faithful pastor, teacher, youth worker, or missionary so much as seeing someone he has led to the Lord turn away from the faith. How much more does such defection grieve the Lord Himself?"
—*John MacArthur*

Reflecting on the Text

9) John R. W. Stott has written: "The church needs people who, in listening to their pastor, listen for the message of Christ, and pastors who, in laboring among the people, look for the image of Christ" (*The Message of Galatians*, [London: InterVarsity, 1968], p. 119, quoted in MacArthur's *Galatians*, p. 120).

In dealing with people (children, neighbors, fellow church members, coworkers), what is your general tone? Are you harsh and unyielding? Or are you gentle and kind? Why?

_____

_____

_____

_____

_____

_____

_____

10) How much is "Christ being formed in you"? What are some tangible evidences of the supernatural, transforming work of the Spirit of God in your life? What are some glaring areas in which you still need to change?

_____

_____

_____

_____

_____

_____

11) What one specific act could you do tomorrow to encourage your pastor, Sunday school teacher, small-group leader, or other spiritual leader?

_____

_____

_____

_____

_____

_____

_____

Recording Your Thoughts

_____

_____

_____

_____

_____

_____

_____

_____

_____

_____

_____

_____

_____

_____

_____

_____

_____

_____

_____

_____

_____

_____

For further study, see the following verses:

Matthew 5:29; 18:5–10   Acts 13:42–50   Philippians 3:4–6
1 John 3:18

Children of Promise

Opening Thought

1) What's your fondest childhood memory?

_____

_____

_____

_____

_____

_____

2) What promise can you remember that a parent made to you when you were very young?

_____

_____

_____

_____

_____

_____

_____

_____

Background of the Passage

When the churches of Galatia were visited by a group of Jewish legalists known as the Judaizers, many believers in Christ were persuaded to participate in Jewish rites and practices in a misguided attempt to earn salvation. For that reason, the apostle Paul wrote the epistle we call Galatians. It was his brilliant, concise attempt to set forth again the simple gospel of salvation by faith alone in Christ alone.

In the passage that is the subject of this lesson, Paul—continuing to contrast grace and law, faith and works—employed an Old Testament story as an analogy or illustration of what he had been teaching. Specifically he compared the two sons of Abraham, Ishmael and Isaac.

Many years after God first promised a son to Abraham, Sarah had not yet conceived. When he was 86 and she 76, Abraham feared that, according to the custom of the day, his chief servant, Eliezer of Damascus, would be his only heir. He cried out to God in despair, and the Lord reaffirmed His original promise, saying, "This one shall not be your heir; but one who will come from your own body, shall be your heir" (Genesis 15:1–4). But when, after several more years, Sarah still had not conceived, she induced Abraham to father a child by her female slave, Hagar.

The birth of that son, whose name was Ishmael, was "according to the flesh," not because it was physical but because the scheme for conception, devised by Sarah and carried out by Abraham, was motivated by purely selfish desires and fulfilled by purely human means.

The birth of Isaac, however, "the son by the free woman," Sarah, was "through the promise." His conception was supernatural, not in the sense that he was conceived directly by the Holy Spirit, as Jesus was, but that the Holy Spirit miraculously enabled Abraham and Sarah to produce a child after she was far past normal childbearing age and had been barren all her life. When Isaac was born, his father was 100 and his mother was 90 (Genesis 17:17; 21:5).

The conception of Ishmael represents humanity's way, the way of the flesh, whereas that of Isaac represents God's way, the way of promise. The first is analogous to the way of religious self-effort and works righteousness. The one is the way of legalism; the other is the way of grace. Ishmael symbolizes those who have had only natural birth and who trust in their own works. Isaac symbolizes those who also have had spiritual birth because they have trusted in the work of Jesus Christ.

Bible Passage

Read 4:21—5:1, noting the key words and definitions to the right of the passage.

Galatians 4:21—5:1

21 *Tell me, you who desire to be under the law, do you not hear the law?*

22 *For it is written that Abraham had two sons: the one by a bondwoman, the other by a freewoman.*

23 *But he who was of the bondwoman was born according to the flesh, and he of the freewoman through promise,*

24 *which things are symbolic. For these are the two covenants: the one from Mount Sinai which gives birth to bondage, which is Hagar—*

25 *for this Hagar is Mount Sinai in Arabia, and corresponds to Jerusalem which now is, and is in bondage with her children—*

26 *but the Jerusalem above is free, which is the mother of us all.*

27 *For it is written:*

"Rejoice, O barren,
You who do not bear!
Break forth and shout,
You who are not in labor!
For the desolate has many more children
Than she who has a husband."

28 *Now we, brethren, as Isaac was, are children of promise.*

29 *But, as he who was born according to the flesh then persecuted him who was born according to the Spirit, even so it is now.*

30 *Nevertheless what does the Scripture say? "Cast out the bondwoman and her son, for the son of the bondwoman shall not be heir with the son of the freewoman."*

two sons (v. 22)—Ishmael, son of Sarah's Egyptian maid Hagar (Genesis 16:1–16), and Isaac, Sarah's son (Genesis 21:1–7)

according to the flesh (v. 23) —Ishmael's birth was motivated by Abraham and Sarah's lack of faith in God's promise and fulfilled by sinful human means.

through promise (v. 23)—God miraculously enabled Abraham and Sarah to have Isaac when Sarah was well past childbearing age and had been barren her entire life.

symbolic (v. 24)—The Greek word was used of a story that conveyed a meaning beyond the literal sense of the words. In this passage, Paul uses historical people and places from the Old Testament to illustrate spiritual truth. This is not an allegory, nor are there any allegories in Scripture—an allegory is a fictional story where real truth is the secret, mysterious, hidden meaning. The story of Abraham, Sarah, Hagar, Ishmael, and Isaac is actual history and has no secret or hidden meaning. Paul uses it only as an illustration to support his contrast between law and grace.

two covenants (v. 24)—Paul uses the two mothers, their two sons, and two locations as a further illustration of two covenants. Hagar, Ishmael, and Mount Sinai (earthly Jerusalem) represent the covenant of law, Sarah, Isaac and

31 *So then, brethren, we are not children of the bond-woman but of the free.*

5:1 *Stand fast therefore in the liberty by which Christ has made us free, and do not be entangled again with a yoke of bondage.*

the heavenly Jerusalem the covenant of promise. The purpose of the Mosaic Covenant was only to show all who were under its demands and condemnation their desperate need for salvation by grace alone (Gal. 3:24); it was never intended to portray the way of salvation. Paul's point is that those, like the Judaizers, who attempt to earn righteousness by keeping the law receive only bondage and condemnation (3:10, 23); while those who partake of salvation by grace—the only way of salvation since Adam's sin—are freed from the law's bondage and condemnation.

Mount Sinai (v. 24)—an appropriate symbol for the old covenant, since it was at Mount Sinai that Moses received the law (Exodus 19)

Hagar (v. 24)—Since she was Sarah's slave (Genesis 16:1), Hagar is a fitting illustration of those under bondage to the law (see Gal.3:5, 21, 23). She was actually associated with Mount Sinai through her son Ishmael, whose descendants settled in that region.

corresponds to Jerusalem (v. 25)—The law was given at Sinai and received its highest expression in the temple worship at Jerusalem. The Jewish people were still in bondage to the law.

Jerusalem above is free (v. 26)—heaven (Heb. 12:18, 22); those who are citizens of heaven (Philippians 3:20) are free from the Mosaic law, works, bondage, and trying endlessly and futilely to please God by the flesh

the mother (v. 26)—Believers are children of the heavenly Jerusalem, the "mother-city" of heaven; in contrast to the slavery of Hagar's children, believers in Christ are free (Gal. 5:1).

children of promise (v. 28)—Just as Isaac inherited the promises made to Abraham, so also are believers the recipients of God's redemptive promises because they are spiritual heirs of Abraham.

he who was born according to the flesh (v. 29)—Ishmael

persecuted him who was born according to the Spirit (v. 29)—Isaac, whom Ishmael mocked at the feast celebrating Isaac's weaning (see Genesis 21:8–9)

Cast out the bondwoman (v. 30)—quoted from Genesis 21:10

Stand fast (5:1)—Stay where you are, Paul asserts, because of the benefit of being free from law and the flesh as a way of salvation and the benefit of the fullness of blessing by grace.

free (5:1)—deliverance from the curse that the law pronounces on the sinner who has been striving unsuccessfully to achieve his own righteousness (Gal. 3:13, 22–26; 4:1–7), but who has now embraced Christ and the salvation granted to him by grace

entangled again (5:1)—better translated "to be burdened by," "to be oppressed by," or "to be subject to," because of its connection with a yoke

yoke of bondage (5:1)—"Yoke" refers to the apparatus used to control a domesticated animal. The Jews referred to the "yoke of the law" as good, the essence of true religion. Paul argued that for those who pursued it as a way of salvation, the law was a yoke of slavery.

Understanding the Text

3) In speaking of two covenants, how can we be sure that Paul was not contrasting two ways of salvation—one for Old Testament saints and another for New Testament believers?

_____

_____

_____

_____

_____

(verses to consider: Galatians 2:16; 3:10–14, 21–22)

4) What does Paul say we enjoy as the children of heavenly Jerusalem?

_____

_____

_____

_____

_____

_____

(verses to consider: Luke 4:18; John 8:36; Romans 6:18, 22–23; 8:2; 2 Corinthians 3:17)

5) What does it mean that, like Isaac, we believers are "children of promise"?

_____

_____

_____

_____

_____

_____

(verses to consider: Genesis 26:1–3; Ephesians 1:3)

Cross-Reference

Read Genesis 21:8–20 (see also Genesis 16:1–16; 21:1–7):

⁸ *So the child grew and was weaned. And Abraham made a great feast on the same day that Isaac was weaned.*

⁹ *And Sarah saw the son of Hagar the Egyptian, whom she had borne to Abraham, scoffing.*

¹⁰ *Therefore she said to Abraham, "Cast out this bondwoman and her son; for the son of this bondwoman shall not be heir with my son, namely with Isaac."*

¹¹ *And the matter was very displeasing in Abraham's sight because of his son.*

¹² *But God said to Abraham, "Do not let it be displeasing in your sight because of the lad or because of your bondwoman. Whatever Sarah has said to you, listen to her voice; for in Isaac your seed shall be called.*

¹³ *Yet I will also make a nation of the son of the bondwoman, because he is your seed."*

14 *So Abraham rose early in the morning, and took bread and a skin of water; and putting it on her shoulder, he gave it and the boy to Hagar, and sent her away. Then she departed and wandered in the Wilderness of Beersheba.*

15 *And the water in the skin was used up, and she placed the boy under one of the shrubs.*

16 *Then she went and sat down across from him at a distance of about a bowshot; for she said to herself, "Let me not see the death of the boy." So she sat opposite him, and lifted her voice and wept.*

17 *And God heard the voice of the lad. Then the angel of God called to Hagar out of heaven, and said to her, "What ails you, Hagar? Fear not, for God has heard the voice of the lad where he is.*

18 *Arise, lift up the lad and hold him with your hand, for I will make him a great nation."*

19 *Then God opened her eyes, and she saw a well of water. And she went and filled the skin with water, and gave the lad a drink.*

20 *So God was with the lad; and he grew and dwelt in the wilderness, and became an archer.*

6) What hints of trouble do you see in the Genesis record of the births and early lives of Ishmael and Isaac?

_____

_____

_____

_____

_____

_____

Exploring the Meaning

7) Read 2 Timothy 3:12. What does this verse mean in light of Galalatians 4:29, which speaks of ancient and present persecution? How would you explain these verses to someone unfamiliar with the Bible?

_____

_____

_____

_____

_____

_____

_____

(verses to consider: Matthew 10:22–25; John 16:2, 33; 1 Peter 4:12–14)

8) Read 2 Thessalonians 1:9. What does this verse say about the destiny of those who attempt to be justified on the basis of keeping the law?

_____

_____

_____

_____

_____

(verses to consider: Matthew 8:12; 22:12–13; 25:30; Luke 13:28)

Summing Up...

"Galatians 4:21—5:1 . . . is an extended series of contrasts between the way of law and the way of grace, the way of works and the way of faith, the way of man and the way of God. Following that same pattern, we also explicitly or implicitly see the contrasts of Hagar/Sarah, Ishmael/Isaac, children of Satan/children of God, commandments/promise, wrath/mercy, bondage/freedom, Old Covenant/New Covenant, Sinai/Zion, present Jerusalem/Jerusalem above, fleshly/spiritual, rejection/inheritance, and lostness/salvation. Throughout this letter, and indeed throughout all of Scripture, such contrasts reflect and demonstrate the contrast of the ages: the way of Satan and the way of God. But in God's ultimate and unchangeable plan, Satan and his way will be destroyed, and only the way of God will remain, forever and ever. Vacillating between the two is unacceptable."—*John MacArthur*

Reflecting on the Text

9) This passage speaks of heaven (that is, "the Jerusalem above"). How should the hope of heaven change the way we live on earth?

_____

_____

_____

_____

_____

_____

10) Paul alludes to persecution in this passage—that just as Ishmael persecuted Isaac, so the children of promise are similarly persecuted today by those who are fleshly and worldly. What kind of persecution have you experienced?

_____

_____

_____

_____

_____

_____

11) What would it look like for you to "stand fast" and to "not be entangled again with a yoke of bondage"? In other words, what specific changes would you need to make in your life?

_____

_____

_____

_____

_____

_____

Recording Your Thoughts

_____

_____

_____

_____

_____

_____

_____

_____

_____

_____

_____

_____

_____

_____

_____

_____

_____

_____

_____

For further study, see the following verses:

Genesis 21:10	Exodus 19	Matthew 11:29–30
Mark 10:30	John 17:14	Romans 7:3; 8:2
Philippians 3:20	Hebrews 12:18, 22	1 Peter 3:14

Called to Freedom

Galatians 5:2–15

Opening Thought

1) You're leading a Bible study class and one of the members says, "My cousin John *used to be* a Christian." How would you respond?

_____

_____

_____

_____

_____

_____

2) Later in that same study, the conversation turns to the subject of Christian freedom. This precipitates a testy exchange between one member who tends to be a bit legalistic and another attendee who participates in many "questionable" behaviors without a seeming twinge of conscience. Suddenly all eyes turn to you for some sort of definitive word of explanation. What do you say?

_____

_____

_____

_____

_____

_____

Background of the Passage

This letter is a succinct treatise on grace from a maligned apostle to a young, confused church.

After defending his apostleship (chapters 1,2) and his message of justification by faith (chapters 3,4), Paul next applied that doctrine to practical Christian living (chapters 5,6), emphasizing that right doctrine should result in right living. His contention is that sanctification should result from justification. The life of genuine faith is more than belief in divine truth; it is also the bearing of divine fruit.

The freedom for which Christ sets us free (5:1) is the freedom to live a life of righteousness in the power of the Holy Spirit. God's standard of holiness has not changed. As Jesus makes clear in the Sermon on the Mount, it requires not simply outward performance but inner perfection. Through His Holy Spirit, believers have the ability to live internal lives of righteousness.

The final two chapters are a portrait of the Spirit-filled life, of the believer's implementing the life of faith under the control and in the energy of the Holy Spirit. The Spirit-filled life thereby becomes in itself a powerful testimony to the power of justification by faith.

In making his appeal for living the Spirit-filled life of freedom rather than reverting to the futile works-bound life of legalistic self-effort, Paul began with a warning against false doctrine (verses 2–6) and false teachers (verses 7–12). Then he explained freedom's grand nature and purpose.

Bible Passage

Read 5:2–15, noting the key words and definitions to the right of the passage.

Galatians 5:2-15

2 *Indeed I, Paul, say to you that if you become circumcised, Christ will profit you nothing.*

3 *And I testify again to every man who becomes circumcised that he is a debtor to keep the whole law.*

circumcised (v. 2)—Paul objected to the notion that circumcision had some spiritual benefit or merit with God and was a prerequisite or necessary component of salvation. Circumcision had meaning in Israel when it was a physical symbol of a cleansed heart (see Jeremiah 9:24–26) and

⁴ *You have become estranged from Christ, you who attempt to be justified by law; you have fallen from grace.*

⁵ *For we through the Spirit eagerly wait for the hope of righteousness by faith.*

⁶ *For in Christ Jesus neither circumcision nor uncircumcision avails anything, but faith working through love.*

⁷ *You ran well. Who hindered you from obeying the truth?*

⁸ *This persuasion does not come from Him who calls you.*

⁹ *A little leaven leavens the whole lump.*

¹⁰ *I have confidence in you, in the Lord, that you will have no other mind; but he who troubles you shall bear his judgment, whoever he is.*

¹¹ *And I, brethren, if I still preach circumcision, why do I still suffer persecution? Then the offense of the cross has ceased.*

¹² *I could wish that those who trouble you would even cut themselves off!*

¹³ *For you, brethren, have been called to liberty; only do not use liberty as an opportunity for the flesh, but through love serve one another.*

¹⁴ *For all the law is fulfilled in one word, even in this: "You shall love your neighbor as yourself."*

¹⁵ *But if you bite and devour one another, beware lest you be consumed by one another!*

served as a reminder of God's covenant of salvation promise (Genesis 17:9–10).

Christ . . . profit you nothing (v. 2)—The atoning sacrifice of Christ cannot benefit anyone who trusts in law and ceremony for salvation.

a debtor to keep the whole law (v. 3)—God's standard is perfect righteousness, and thus a failure to keep only one part of the law falls short of the standard.

estranged from Christ . . . fallen from grace (v. 4)—The Greek word for "estranged" means "to be separated" or "to be severed." The word for "fallen" means "to lose one's grasp on something." Paul's clear meaning is that any attempt to be justified by the law is to reject salvation by grace alone through faith alone; those once exposed to the gracious truth of the gospel who then turn their backs on Christ and seek to be justified by the law are separated from Christ and lose all prospects of God's gracious salvation. Their desertion of Christ and the gospel proves that their faith was never genuine.

the hope of righteousness by faith (v. 5)—Christians already possess the imputed righteousness of Christ, but they still await the completed and perfected righteousness that is yet to come at glorification.

neither circumcision nor uncircumcision avails anything (v. 6)—Nothing done or not done in the flesh, even religious ceremony, makes any difference in one's relationship to God. What is external is immaterial and worthless, unless it reflects genuine internal righteousness.

faith working through love (v. 6)—Saving faith proves its genuine character by works of love; the one who lives by faith is internally motivated by love for God and Christ, which supernaturally issues forth in reverent worship, genuine obedience, and self-sacrificing love for others.

You ran well (v. 7)—Paul compares the Galatians' life of faith with a race. They had a good beginning—they had received the gospel message by faith and had begun to live their Christian lives by faith as well.

obeying the truth (v. 7)—a reference to believers' true way of living, including both their response to the true gospel in salvation (see Acts 6:7; Romans 2:8; 6:17; 2 Thessalonians 1:8) and their consequent response to obey the Word of God in sanctification. Paul wrote more about salvation and sanctification being a matter of obedience in Romans 1:5; 6:16–17; 16:26. The legalistic influence of the Judaizers prevented the unsaved from responding in faith to the gospel of grace and true believers from living by faith.

This persuasion (v. 8)—salvation by works. God does not promote legalism; any doctrine that claims His gracious work is insufficient to save is false.

leaven (v. 9)—a common axiomatic saying (see 1 Corinthians 5:6) regarding the influence of yeast in dough. Leaven is often used in Scripture to denote sin (Matthew 16:6, 12) because of its permeating power.

confidence in you (v. 10)—Paul expresses encouraging assurance that the Lord will be faithful to keep His own from falling into gross heresy; they will persevere and be preserved (Jude 24).

judgment (v. 10)—All false teachers will incur strict and devastating eternal condemnation.

still preach circumcision (v. 11)—Apparently the Judaizers had falsely claimed that Paul agreed with their teaching; he makes the point, however, that if he was preaching circumcision as necessary for salvation, why were the Judaizers persecuting him instead of supporting him?

offense of the cross (v. 11)—The Greek word for "offense" can mean "trap," "snare," or "stumbling block." Any offer of salvation that strips a person of the opportunity to earn it by his own merit breeds opposition (see Romans 9:33).

cut themselves off (v. 12)—Better translated "mutilate themselves," the Greek word was often used of castration, such as in the cult of Cybele, whose priests were self-made eunuchs. Paul's ironic point is that since the Judaizers were so insistent on circumcision as a means of pleasing God, they should go to the extreme of religious devotion and mutilate themselves.

opportunity for the flesh (v. 13)—The Greek word for "opportunity" was often used to refer to a central base of military operations (see Romans 7:8). In the context, "flesh" refers to the sinful inclinations of fallen humanity; the freedom Christians have is not a base from which they can sin freely and without consequence.

serve one another (v. 13)—Christian freedom is not for selfish fulfillment but for serving others.

all the law (v. 14)—The ethics of the former Old Testament law are the same as those of the New Testament gospel, as indicated in the quote from Leviticus 19:18. When a Christian genuinely loves others, he or she fulfills all the moral requirements of the former Mosaic law concerning them; this is the ruling principle of Christian freedom (Gal. 5:6, 13).

bite and devour one another (v. 15)—The imagery is of wild animals savagely attacking and killing each other—a graphic picture of what happens in the spiritual realm when believers do not love and serve each other.

Understanding the Text

3) Did Paul view circumcision as an inherently bad practice? How do you know? (See 5:6.)

_____

_____

_____

_____

_____

(verses to consider: Deuteronomy 30:6; Jeremiah 4:4; Acts 16:1–3; Philippians 3:3–5)

4) What does Paul mean that the Galatians "ran well"?

_____

_____

_____

_____

_____

(verses to consider: 1 Corinthians 9:24–27)

5) What does Paul teach in Galatians 5:10 about "the perseverance of the saints"?

_____

_____

_____

_____

_____

(verses to consider: John 6:39–40; 10:28–29; Romans 8:31–39; Philippians 1:6, 7)

6) How does Paul summarize the law? Whose words is he echoing here?

_____

_____

_____

_____

_____

(verses to consider: Matthew 22:36–40; Romans 7:12; 8:4; James 2:8–10)

Cross-Reference

Read Romans 14:1–15:

¹ *Receive one who is weak in the faith, but not to disputes over doubtful things.*
² *For one believes he may eat all things, but he who is weak eats only vegetables.*
³ *Let not him who eats despise him who does not eat, and let not him who does not eat judge him who eats; for God has received him.*
⁴ *Who are you to judge another's servant? To his own master he stands or falls. Indeed, he will be made to stand, for God is able to make him stand.*
⁵ *One person esteems one day above another; another esteems every day alike. Let each be fully convinced in his own mind.*
⁶ *He who observes the day, observes it to the Lord; and he who does not observe the day, to the Lord he does not observe it. He who eats, eats to the Lord, for he gives God thanks; and he who does not eat, to the Lord he does not eat, and gives God thanks.*
⁷ *For none of us lives to himself, and no one dies to himself.*
⁸ *For if we live, we live to the Lord; and if we die, we die to the Lord. Therefore, whether we live or die, we are the Lord's.*
⁹ *For to this end Christ died and rose and lived again, that He might be Lord of both the dead and the living.*
¹⁰ *But why do you judge your brother? Or why do you show contempt for your brother? For we shall all stand before the judgment seat of Christ.*
¹¹ *For it is written:*
"As I live, says the LORD,

Every knee shall bow to Me,
And every tongue shall confess to God."

¹² *So then each of us shall give account of himself to God.*

¹³ *Therefore let us not judge one another anymore, but rather resolve this, not to put a stumbling block or a cause to fall in our brother's way.*

¹⁴ *I know and am convinced by the Lord Jesus that there is nothing unclean of itself; but to him who considers anything to be unclean, to him it is unclean.*

¹⁵ *Yet if your brother is grieved because of your food, you are no longer walking in love. Do not destroy with your food the one for whom Christ died.*

7) What is the purpose of Christian freedom?

_____

_____

_____

_____

_____

_____

Exploring the Meaning

8) Read 1 John 2:19. How does this passage address the idea of deserting Christ and the gospel that Paul discusses in Galatians 5:4?

_____

_____

_____

_____

_____

_____

_____

(verses to consider: Luke 8:13–14; Hebrews 6:4–6)

9) Read Romans 2:25–29. How does this passage contribute to Paul's argument in Galatians 5:5–6 that external religious actions are meaningless without an internal change?

_____

_____

_____

_____

_____

_____

_____

_____

Summing Up...

"Someone has pictured legalism and libertinism as two parallel streams that run between earth and heaven. The stream of legalism is clear, sparkling, and pure; but its waters run so deep and furiously that no one can enter it without being drowned or smashed on the rocks of its harsh demands. The stream of libertinism, by contrast, is relatively quiet and still, and crossing it seems easy and attractive. But its waters are so contaminated with poisons and pollutants that to try to cross it is also certain death. Both streams are uncrossable and deadly, one because of impossible moral and spiritual demands, the other because of moral and spiritual filth.

"But spanning those two deadly streams is the bridge of the gospel of Jesus Christ, the only passage from earth to heaven. The two streams lead to death because they are man's ways. The gospel leads to life because it is God's way."—_John MacArthur_

Reflecting on the Text

10) This lesson speaks of the importance of "faith working through love."

What are some specific examples of this in your life? What are some areas in which you need to see more evidence of a loving faith?"

_____

_____

_____

_____

_____

_____

11) If Paul were to write a letter to you personally, would he say, "You were running well" or would he say, "You are running well"? Why?

_____

_____

_____

_____

_____

12) Over and over, the New Testament calls believers to serve one another. How would you grade yourself in the area of service? Why?

_____

_____

_____

_____

_____

Recording Your Thoughts

_____

_____

_____

_____

_____

_____

_____

_____

_____

_____

_____

_____

_____

_____

_____

_____

_____

_____

_____

_____

_____

For further study, see the following verses:

Deuteronomy 6:5   Matthew 22:37–40   Luke 22:24–27
Romans 3:24; 8:18, 21   Romans 13:8–10; 15:3   Philippians 2:5–7
1 Peter 1:22   2 Peter 2:2; 3:9

Walking by the Spirit

Opening Thought

1) What do you think of the following summaries of the Christian life? How would you describe each approach? Are they biblical phrases or not?

"Let go and let God!"

"It's all of Him, and none of us."

"Keep seeking more of the Spirit-fresh anointings, new out pourings."

"Just say no to sin and yes to God."

"Surrender completely to Jesus."

"Be sold out to Christ."

"Fight the good fight and run the race!"

"Give the Master charge of your life."

"Just do what the Bible says."

"Practice the presence of God."

"Walk with the Lord."

2) How would you summarize the Christian life?

_____

_____

_____

Background of the Passage

Following Paul's planting of churches in the Galatian region of Asia Minor, a group of Jewish legalists known as the Judaizers had arrived. These intensely religious folk had confused the Galatian believers by denigrating Paul and his message and by promoting an eclectic spirituality of Jesus plus Judaism. Paul wrote Galatians to vindicate his authority and message as an apostle and to lay out again the distinction between law and grace, faith and works.

The final two chapters provide a practical guidebook to how the gracious gospel should make a difference in a Christian's everyday life. Just as Jesus Christ is the primary Person behind justification, the Holy Spirit is the primary Person behind sanctification. A believer can no more sanctify himself than he could have saved himself in the first place. He cannot live the Christian life by his own resources any more than he could have saved himself by his own resources.

In its most profound yet simple definition, the faithful Christian life is lived under the direction and by the power of the Spirit. That is the theme of 5:16–25, which tells believers to "walk by the Spirit" (verses 16, 25) and to be "led by the Spirit" (verse 18). The opening paragraph (verses 16–18) of this section introduces the passage by setting forth the command and the conflict of the Spirit-led life.

In short, Paul's argument is that the Holy Spirit makes the life of faith work. Were it not for the indwelling power of the Holy Spirit, the life of faith would be no more spiritually productive or acceptable to God than the life of law.

Bible Passage

Read 5:16–26, noting the key words and definitions to the right of the passage.

Galatians 5:16–26

16 *I say then: Walk in the Spirit, and you shall not fulfill the lust of the flesh.*

17 *For the flesh lusts against the Spirit, and the Spirit against the flesh; and these are contrary to one another, so that you do not do the things that you wish.*

Walk in the Spirit (v. 16)—All believers have the presence of the indwelling Holy Spirit (see Romans 8:9; 1 Corinthians 6:19–20) as the personal power for living to please God. The form of the Greek verb translated "walk" indicates continuous action, or a habitual lifestyle. Walking also implies progress; as

18 *But if you are led by the Spirit, you are not under the law.*

19 *Now the works of the flesh are evident, which are: adultery, fornication, uncleanness, lewdness,*

20 *idolatry, sorcery, hatred, contentions, jealousies, outbursts of wrath, selfish ambitions, dissensions, heresies,*

21 *envy, murders, drunkenness, revelries, and the like; of which I tell you beforehand, just as I also told you in time past, that those who practice such things will not inherit the kingdom of God.*

22 *But the fruit of the Spirit is love, joy, peace, long-suffering, kindness, goodness, faithfulness,*

23 *gentleness, self-control. Against such there is no law.*

24 *And those who are Christ's have crucified the flesh with its passions and desires.*

25 *If we live in the Spirit, let us also walk in the Spirit.*

26 *Let us not become conceited, provoking one another, envying one another.*

a believer submits to the Spirit's control—that is, responds in obedience to the simple commands of Scripture—he or she grows in his or her spiritual life.

the flesh (v. 16)—This is not simply the physical body. It includes the mind, will, and emotions, which are all subject to sin, and refers, in general to our unredeemed humanness.

contrary to one another (v. 17)—The flesh opposes the work of the Spirit and leads the believer toward sinful behavior that he or she would not otherwise be compelled to do.

led by the Spirit . . . not under the law (v. 18)—Take your choice; these are mutually exclusive. Either you live by the power of the Holy Spirit, which results in righteous behavior and spiritual attitudes (Gal. 3:22–29), or you live by the law, which can only produce unrighteous behavior and attitudes (verses 19–21).

now the works of the flesh . . . (vv. 19–21)—These sins characterize all unredeemed humankind, though not every person manifests all these sins nor exhibits them to the same degree. Paul's list, which is not exhaustive, encompasses three areas of human life: sex, religion, and human relationships.

evident (v. 19)—The flesh manifests itself in obvious and certain ways.

fornication (v. 19)—The Greek word is *porneia*, from which the English word "pornography" comes. It refers to all illicit sexual activity, including (but not limited to) adultery, premarital sex, homosexuality, bestiality, incest, and prostitution.

lewdness (v. 19)—The word originally referred to any excessive behavior or lack of restraint, but eventually became associated with sexual excess and indulgence.

sorcery (v. 20)—This Greek word, from which our English word "pharmacy" comes, originally referred to medicines in general but eventually only to mood- and mind-altering drugs, as well as the occult, witchcraft, and magic. Many pagan religious practices required the use of these drugs to aid in the communication with deities.

contentions . . . heresies (v. 20)—Many of these sins manifested in the area of human relationships have to do with some form of anger: "Hatred" results in "contentions" (strife); "jealousies" (hateful resentment) result in "outbursts of wrath" (sudden, unrestrained expressions of hostility); the next four represent animosity between individuals and groups.

drunkenness, revelries (v. 21)—probably a specific reference to the orgies that characterized pagan, idolatrous worship; generally, it refers to all rowdy, boisterous, and crude behavior.

practice (v. 21)—Here is the key word in Paul's warning; the sense of this Greek verb describes continual, habitual action. Although believers undoubtedly can commit these sins, those people whose basic character is summed up in the uninterrupted and unrepentant practice of them cannot belong to God.

will not inherit the kingdom of God (v. 21)—The unregenerate are barred from entering the spiritual kingdom of redeemed people over whom Christ now rules, and they will be excluded from His millennial kingdom and the eternal state of blessing that follows it.

fruit of the Spirit (v. 22)—the Spirit of God. The Spirit produces fruit which consists of nine characteristics or attitudes that are inextricably linked with each and are commanded of believers throughout the New Testament.

love (v. 22)—One of several Greek words for love, *agape*, refers to the love of choice, not an emotional affection, physical attraction, or a familial bond, but the respect, devotion, and affection that lead to willing, self-sacrificial service.

joy (v. 22)—a happiness based on unchanging divine promises and eternal spiritual realities. It is the sense of well-being experienced by one who knows all is well between himself or herself and the Lord; it is not the result of favorable circumstances, and even occurs when those circumstances are the most painful and severe. Joy is a gift from God, and as such, believers are not to manufacture it but to delight in the blessing they already possess.

peace (v. 22)—the inner calm that results from confidence in one's saving relationship with Christ. The verb form denotes binding together and is reflected in the expression "having it all together"; like joy, peace is not related to one's circumstances (John 14:27; Romans 8:28; Philippians 4:6–7, 9).

longsuffering (v. 22)—the patience to endure injuries inflicted by others and the willingness to accept irritating or painful situations (Ephesians 4:2; Colossians 3:12; 1 Timothy 1:15–16)

kindness (v. 22)—tender concern for others, reflected in a desire to treat others gently, just as the Lord treats all believers (Matthew 11:28, 29; 19:13–14; 2 Timothy 2:24)

goodness (v. 22)—moral and spiritual excellence manifested in active kindness (Romans 5:7); believers are commanded to exemplify goodness (6:10; 2 Thessalonians 1:11).

faithfulness (v. 22)—loyalty and trustworthiness (Lamentations 3:22; Philippians 2:7–9; 1 Thessalonians 5:24; Revelation 2:10)

gentleness (v. 23)—Better translated "meekness," this is a humble and gentle attitude that is patiently submissive in every offense, while having no desire for revenge or retribution. In the New Testament, it is used to describe three attitudes: submission to the will of God (Colossians 3:12), teachability (James 1:21), and consideration of others (Ephesians 4:2).

self-control (v. 23)—This refers to restraining passions and appetites (1 Corinthians 9:25; 2 Peter 1:5–6).

no law (v. 23)—When a Christian walks by the Spirit and manifests His fruit, he or she needs no external law to produce the attitudes and behavior that please God (see Romans 8:4).

have crucified the flesh (v. 24)—one of four uses of "crucified" that does not refer to Christ's crucifixion. Paul states that the flesh has been executed, yet the spiritual battle still rages in the believer (Romans 7:14–25): Paul's use looks back to the cross of Christ, where the death of the flesh and its power to reign over believers was actually accomplished (Romans 6:1–11): Christians must wait until their glorification before they are finally rid of their unredeemed humanness (Romans 8:23), yet by walking in the Spirit they can please God in this world.

Understanding the Text

3) Is Paul arguing in this passage that those who commit these sins prove they are not really Christians? Why or why not? What Scripture would you use to support your answer?

_____

_____

_____

_____

_____

_____

4) What is unique about the love produced by the Spirit of God?

_____

_____

_____

_____

_____

(verses to consider: John 15:13; Romans 5:8; 1 John 3:16–17)

5) How would you define Christian joy? In what ways is it different from the emotion known as happiness?

_____

_____

_____

_____

_____

_____

(verses to consider: John 16:20–22; Romans 14:17; 1 Peter 1:8)

Cross-Reference

Read Romans 1:24–32:

²⁴ *Therefore God also gave them up to uncleanness, in the lusts of their hearts, to dishonor their bodies among themselves,*

²⁵ *who exchanged the truth of God for the lie, and worshiped and served the creature rather than the Creator, who is blessed forever. Amen.*

²⁶ *For this reason God gave them up to vile passions. For even their women exchanged the natural use for what is against nature.*

²⁷ *Likewise also the men, leaving the natural use of the woman, burned in their lust for one another, men with men committing what is shameful, and receiving in themselves the penalty of their error which was due.*

²⁸ *And even as they did not like to retain God in their knowledge, God gave them over to a debased mind, to do those things which are not fitting;*

²⁹ *being filled with all unrighteousness, sexual immorality, wickedness, covetousness, maliciousness; full of envy, murder, strife, deceit, evil-mindedness; they are whisperers,*

³⁰ *backbiters, haters of God, violent, proud, boasters, inventors of evil things, disobedient to parents,*

³¹ *undiscerning, untrustworthy, unloving, unforgiving, unmerciful;*

³² *who, knowing the righteous judgment of God, that those who practice such things are deserving of death, not only do the same but also approve of those who practice them.*

6) How does this list from Romans 1 compare with Paul's list of fleshly activities in Galatians 5?

_____

_____

_____

_____

_____

_____

_____

Exploring the Meaning

7) Read Romans 6:6. What does it mean that our flesh has been crucified?

_____

_____

_____

_____

_____

_____

(verses to consider: Romans 6:7–14)

8) Read Ephesians 5:18. What insight does this verse shed on the idea of walking by the Spirit?

_____

_____

_____

_____

_____

_____

_____

(verses to consider: Romans 8:13; Colossians 3:16)

Summing Up...

"Because believers have new life in Jesus Christ, they should also have a new way of life."—*John MacArthur*

Reflecting on the Text

9) Many followers of Jesus look for and pursue a dramatic experience or sudden insight they think will help them attain spiritual maturity and consistency. Based on your study in this lesson, why is this an erroneous understanding of the Christian life?

_____

_____

_____

_____

_____

_____

10) How would you describe/define "the flesh"? In what specific areas does your flesh seem to rear its ugly head most often?

_____

_____

_____

_____

_____

_____

_____

11) How do you know when you are walking in the Spirit? Is there a way to know for sure?

_____

_____

_____

_____

_____

_____

12) If a young Christian came to you and said, "I don't see much of the fruit of the Spirit in my life," what counsel would you give?

_____

_____

_____

_____

_____

_____

Recording Your Thoughts

_____

_____

_____

_____

_____

_____

_____

_____

_____

_____

For further study, see the following verses:

Romans 7:5, 14–25; 8:23   1 Corinthians 6:9–10; 15:56   Philippians 4:4

A Grace-filled Life

Opening Thought

1) The leaders of your church are exercising "church discipline" on a man in your local body who has left his wife and family for his secretary. Specifically they are telling him he has no biblical grounds for dissolving his marriage, that he is guilty of adultery, and that if he will not repent and return, he will be removed from the church's membership.

A number of church members are outraged that the leadership could be so "nosy and judgmental"; others are glad to see that their leaders have enough backbone to stand up to declining morals and blatant sin.

What do you think?

_____

_____

_____

_____

2) Is this decision on the part of the church leaders (a) harsh; (b) loving; (c) intolerant; (d) strange; (e) none of the above? Why?

_____

_____

_____

_____

_____

Background of the Passage

The end of Paul's letter to the Galatian churches carries the same weight of seriousness, urgency, and indignation as the rest of it. Both the beginning and end (1:3; 6:18) commend readers to God's grace and express Paul's deep concern for the spiritual welfare of those to whom he was writing. But Paul took no time for the personal amenities found in most of his other letters. It is almost as if the courier were standing at the door, waiting for Paul to finish writing so he could rush the letter on its way.

Following brief instructions about restoring a sinning brother (5:26—6:6) and the inviolable spiritual law of sowing and reaping (6:7–10), Paul contrasted those who would glory in the flesh (6:11–13) with those who glory only in the cross (6:14–18). Except for the closing benediction (verse 18), verses 11 to the end are largely a parting salvo against the Judaizers, whose heretical activities prompted the letter in the first place. They were teaching the spurious, human-made gospel (which was no gospel at all, 1:6–7) of salvation by works and of living under the government of law, in complete contradiction to the divine gospel of salvation by grace and living by the Spirit that Paul had preached when he ministered in Galatia.

Most of the letter has been spent condemning the false teaching of the Judaizers. Here, at the end, Paul condemned their motives for teaching their legalistic perversion of the gospel, declaring that they were motivated by religious pride, by cowardice, and by hypocrisy. Paul, on the other hand, gloried in the cross because it was the sacrifice of the Lord Jesus Christ on the cross that was the source of his and every believer's righteousness and acceptance before God. Only the cross is able to bring an end to humankind's hopeless frustration in pursuing God through works.

Bible Passage

Read 6:1–18, noting the key words and definitions to the right of the passage.

Galatians 6:1–18

¹ *Brethren, if a man is overtaken in any trespass, you who are spiritual restore such a one in a spirit of gentleness, considering yourself lest you also be tempted.*

overtaken (v. 1)—literally "caught," which may imply the person was actually seen committing the sin, or that he was caught or snared by the sin itself

² *Bear one another's burdens, and so fulfill the law of Christ.*

³ *For if anyone thinks himself to be something, when he is nothing, he deceives himself.*

⁴ *But let each one examine his own work, and then he will have rejoicing in himself alone, and not in another.*

⁵ *For each one shall bear his own load.*

⁶ *Let him who is taught the word share in all good things with him who teaches.*

⁷ *Do not be deceived, God is not mocked; for whatever a man sows, that he will also reap.*

⁸ *For he who sows to his flesh will of the flesh reap corruption, but he who sows to the Spirit will of the Spirit reap everlasting life.*

⁹ *And let us not grow weary while doing good, for in due season we shall reap if we do not lose heart.*

¹⁰ *Therefore, as we have opportunity, let us do good to all, especially to those who are of the household of faith.*

¹¹ *See with what large letters I have written to you with my own hand!*

¹² *As many as desire to make a good showing in the flesh, these would compel you to be circumcised, only that they may not suffer persecution for the cross of Christ.*

¹³ *For not even those who are circumcised keep the law, but they desire to have you circumcised that they may boast in your flesh.*

¹⁴ *But God forbid that I should boast except in the cross of our Lord Jesus Christ, by whom the world has been crucified to me, and I to the world.*

¹⁵ *For in Christ Jesus neither circumcision nor uncircumcision avails anything, but a new creation.*

¹⁶ *And as many as walk according to this rule, peace and mercy be upon them, and upon the Israel of God.*

¹⁷ *From now on let no one trouble me, for I bear in my body the marks of the Lord Jesus.*

¹⁸ *Brethren, the grace of our Lord Jesus Christ be with your spirit. Amen.*

you . . . spiritual (v. 1)—those believers who are walking in the Spirit, filled with the Spirit and evidencing the fruit of the Spirit (Gal. 5:22–23)

restore (v. 1)—Sometimes used metaphorically of settling disputes or arguments, it literally means "to mend" or "repair," and was used of setting a broken bone or repairing a dislocated limb. The basic process of restoration is outlined in Matthew 18:15–20.

considering (v. 1)—also "looking to, observing"; the Greek form strongly emphasizes a continual, diligent attentiveness

Bear one another's burdens (v. 2)—"Burdens" are extra heavy loads, which here represent difficulties or problems people have trouble dealing with. "Bear" connotes carrying something with endurance.

the law of Christ (v. 2)—the law of love which fulfills the entire law

examine (v. 4)—literally "to approve something after testing it"; believers first must be sure their lives are right with God before giving spiritual help to others

have rejoicing in himself (v. 4)—Believers should rejoice or boast in the Lord only for what God has done in him or her (see 2 Corinthians 10:12–18), not for what he or she supposedly has accomplished compared to other believers.

bear his own load (v. 5)—This is not a contradiction to verse 2. "Load" has no connotation of difficulty; it refers to life's routine obligations and each believer's ministry calling. God requires faithfulness in meeting those responsibilities.

all good things (v. 6)— Although this expression could refer to material compensation, the context suggests that Paul is referring to the spiritually and morally excellent things learned from the Word, in which they fellowship together. Paul uses this same term to describe the gospel (Romans 10:15).

whatever a man sows . . . reap (v. 7)—This agricultural principle, applied metaphorically to the moral and spiritual realm, is universally true. This law is a form of God's wrath.

sows to his flesh (v. 8)—Here it means pandering to the flesh's evil desires.

corruption (v. 8)—from the Greek word for degeneration, as in decaying food; sin always corrupts and, when left unchecked, always makes a person progressively worse in character (see Romans 6:23)

sows to the Spirit (v. 8)—to walk by the Holy Spirit

everlasting life (v. 8)—This expression describes not only a life that endures forever but, primarily, the highest quality of living that one can experience (see Ephesians 1:3, 18).

opportunity (v. 10)—The Greek word is *kairos* and refers to a distinct, fixed time period, rather than occasional moments. Paul's point is that the believer's entire life provides the unique privilege by which he or she can serve others in Christ's name.

especially . . . the household of faith (v. 10)—Our love for fellow Christians is the primary test of our love for God.

with what large letters (v. 11)—This can be interpreted in two ways: (1) Paul's poor eyesight forced him to use large letters (Gal. 4:13, 15); or (2) instead of the normal cursive style of writing used by professional scribes, Paul used the large, block letters (frequently employed in public notices) to emphasize the letter's content rather than its form. It was a visible picture that contrasted his concern with the content of the gospel for the Judaizers' only concern: appearances. The expression served as a transition to his concluding remarks.

I have written . . . my own hand (v. 11)—As a good translation of the Greek verb, this indicates that Paul wrote the entire letter by his own hand, not merely penning a brief statement at the end of dictation to a secretary as he did other times (see 1 Corinthians 16:21; 2 Thessalonians 3:17). Paul wrote this letter himself to make sure the Galatians knew he—not some forger—was writing it and to personalize the document, given the importance and severity of its contents.

good showing (v. 12)—The Judaizers were motivated by religious pride and wanted to impress others with their external piety (see Matthew 6:1–7).

may not suffer persecution (v. 12)—The Judaizers were more concerned about their personal safety than correct doctrine. By adhering more to the Mosaic law than to the gospel of Jesus, they hoped to avoid social and financial ostracism from other Jews and maintain their protected status as Jews within the Roman Empire.

circumcised (v. 13)—specifically, in this case, the Judaizers (see Acts 11:2)

boast in your flesh (v. 13)—They zealously worked to win Gentile converts to the law so they could brag about their effective proselytizing.

boast except in the cross (v. 14)—The Greek word for "boast" is a basic expression of praise, unlike the English word, which necessarily includes the aspect of pride. Paul glories and rejoices in the sacrifice of Jesus Christ.

the world (v. 14)—the evil, Satanic system

crucified to me, and I to the world (v. 14)—The world is spiritually dead to believers, and they are dead to the world.

a new creation (v. 15)—the new birth

peace and mercy (v. 16)—the results of salvation: "peace" is the believer's new relationship to God (Romans 5:1; 8:6; Colossians 3:15), and "mercy" is the forgiveness of all his sins and the setting aside of God's judgment (Psalm 25:6; Daniel 9:18; Matthew 5:7; Luke 1:50; Romans 12:1; Ephesians 2:4; Titus 3:5)

Israel of God (v. 16)—all Jewish believers in Christ, that is, those who are both physical and spiritual descendants of Abraham (see Romans 2:28–29; 9:6–7; Galatians 3:7,18)

marks (v. 17)—the physical results of persecution (scars, wounds, etc.) that identified Paul as one who had suffered for the Lord (see Acts 16:22; 2 Corinthians 1:5; 4:10; Colossians 1:24)

Understanding the Text

3) What is involved in restoring a sinning Christian brother or sister?

_____

_____

_____

_____

_____

_____

(verses to consider: Matthew 7:3–5; 18:15–17; Romans 15:1–2; 1 Thessalonians 5:14; Hebrews 12:3–11)

4) What does Paul mean when he commands each believer to "bear his own load"?

_____

_____

_____

_____

_____

_____

5) How would you explain the law of sowing and reaping in your own terms—say, to a child?

_____

_____

_____

_____

_____

(verses to consider: Job 4:8; Proverbs 1:31–33; Hosea 10:12)

6) What was Paul's point in contrasting boasting in the flesh with boasting in the cross?

_____

_____

_____

_____

_____

(verses to consider: Romans 8:1–3; 1 Corinthians 2:2; 1 Peter 2:24)

Cross Reference

Read 1 Corinthians 5:1–13:

¹ *It is actually reported that there is sexual immorality among you, and such sexual immorality as is not even named among the Gentiles—that a man has his father's wife!*

² *And you are puffed up, and have not rather mourned, that he who has done this deed might be taken away from among you.*

³ *For I indeed, as absent in body but present in spirit, have already judged (as though I were present) him who has so done this deed.*

⁴ *In the name of our Lord Jesus Christ, when you are gathered together, along with my spirit, with the power of our Lord Jesus Christ,*

⁵ *deliver such a one to Satan for the destruction of the flesh, that his spirit may be saved in the day of the Lord Jesus.*

⁶ *Your glorying is not good. Do you not know that a little leaven leavens the whole lump?*

⁷ *Therefore purge out the old leaven, that you may be a new lump, since you truly are unleavened. For indeed Christ, our Passover, was sacrificed for us.*

⁸ *Therefore let us keep the feast, not with old leaven, nor with the leaven of malice and wickedness, but with the unleavened bread of sincerity and truth.*

⁹ *I wrote to you in my epistle not to keep company with sexually immoral people.*

¹⁰ *Yet I certainly did not mean with the sexually immoral people of this world, or with the covetous, or extortioners, or idolaters, since then you would need to go out of the world.*

¹¹ *But now I have written to you not to keep company with anyone named a brother, who is sexually immoral, or covetous, or an idolater, or a reviler, or a drunkard, or an extortioner—not even to eat with such a person.*

¹² *For what have I to do with judging those also who are outside? Do you not judge those who are inside?*

¹³ *But those who are outside God judges. Therefore "put away from yourselves the evil person."*

7) What extra insight does this chapter provide about the whole process of church discipline?

_____

_____

_____

_____

_____

Exploring the Meaning

8) Read John 13:34–35. Why is our demonstrated love for fellow Christians so important?

_____

_____

_____

_____

_____

_____

_____

(verses to consider: Romans 12:10–13; 1 John 4:20–21)

9) Read Philippians 3:20–21. What is the believer's true relationship with the world?

_____

_____

_____

_____

_____

_____

_____

(verses to consider: Romans 6:2–10; Galatians 2:20; 1 John 2:15–16; 5:4–5)

Summing Up...

"The most important pursuit for all Christians, individually and corporately, is holiness. The first mission of the church is to honor and glorify God, and He can be honored and glorified by His children only as they grow to be like Him in character. Although evangelism is the cutting edge of the church's ministry, holiness is the only foundation on which effective evangelism or any other ministry can be built. The supreme priority of the church is holiness, purity of inward life. God can accomplish whatever he desires through a believer or a church that is holy, but He can do little through one that is not."—*John MacArthur*

Reflecting on the Text

10) Most instances of correcting a Christian brother or sister never reach the church discipline stage. That's because according to the process outlined in Matthew 18, the first step is a one-on-one confrontation. Have you ever been gently confronted by another believer? What happened?

_____

_____

_____

_____

_____

11) Is there anyone in your immediate circle who needs to be lovingly corrected because of sin?

_____

_____

_____

_____

_____

12) In what areas of your life and ministry are you tempted to give up out of weariness and out of a sense that your efforts aren't making a difference? What counsel would Paul give you?

_____

_____

_____

_____

_____

_____

13) When was the last time you pondered the mystery and majesty of all that the cross of Christ represents? How can you express your gratitude to God for His amazing blessings that were poured out on you because of the cross?

_____

_____

_____

_____

_____

_____

Recording Your Thoughts

_____

_____

_____

_____

_____

_____

_____

For further study, see the following verses:

Psalm 51:12	John 3:3; 8:31; 10:10	John 13:34; 15:7
Acts 10:45; 14:19	Romans 1:18; 7:18; 8:23	Romans 12:1–2;
Romans 13:8, 10	1 Corinthians 1:31	2 Corinthians 2:7; 5:17
2 Corinthians 11:25	Ephesians 5:18–20	Colossians 2:6; 3:16
Colossians 4:18	2 Thessalonians 3:15	Hebrews 9:11
1 John 5:19		

Additional Notes

Additional Notes

The MacArthur Bible Collection

John MacArthur, General Editor

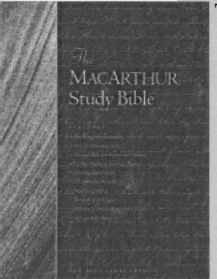

The MacArthur Study Bible

From the moment you pick it up, you'll know it's a classic. Featuring the word-for-word accuracy of the New King James Version, *The MacArthur Study Bible* is perfect for serious study. Pastor/teacher John MacArthur has compiled more than 20,000 study notes, a 200-page topical index and numerous charts, maps, outlines, and articles to create *The MacArthur Study Bible*. This Bible has been crafted with the finest materials in a variety of handsome bindings, including hardcover and indexed bonded leather. Winner of "The 1998 Study Bible of the Year Award."

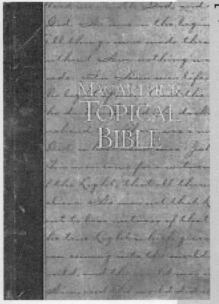

The MacArthur Topical Bible

In the excellent tradition of *Nave's Topical Bible,* this newly created reference book incorporates thousands of topics and ideas, both traditional and contemporary, for believers today and in the new millennium. Carefully researched and prepared by Dr. John MacArthur and the faculty of Masters Seminary, *The MacArthur Topical Bible* will quickly become the reference of choice of all serious Bible students. Using the New King James translation, this Bible is arranged alphabetically by topic and is completely cross-referenced. This exhaustive resource is an indispensible tool for the topical study of God's Word.

The MacArthur Bible Studies

These first four study guides in a 16-volume set from noted Bible scholar John MacArthur take readers on a journey through biblical texts to discover what lies beneath the surface, focusing on meaning and context, and then reflecting on the explored passage or concept. With probing questions that guide the reader toward application, as well as ample space for journaling, *The MacArthur Bible Studies* are an invaluable tool for Bible students of all ages.